Down Under

Understanding the New Zealand Dolphin

LIZ SLOOTEN & STEVE DAWSON

OTAGO

Without substantial contributions from the New Zealand Whale and Dolphin Trust and the University of Otago, this book would probably never have been written. More detailed information about research on the New Zealand dolphin can be found at: www.whaledolphintrust.org.nz

Tax-exempt donations for research and conservation efforts can be made at: www.whaledolphintrust.org.nz

Published by Otago University Press
Level 1 / 398 Cumberland Street
PO Box 56, Dunedin, New Zealand
F: 64 3 479 8385. E: university.press@otago.ac.nz
W: www.otago.ac.nz/press

Publisher: Wendy Harrex
Design: Fiona Moffat
Photographs: Steve Dawson unless indicated
Index: Diane Lowther

Printed in New Zealand by
Printlink Ltd, Wellington

CONTENTS

WHY THIS BOOK?

NEW ZEALAND DOLPHINS, also known as Hector's dolphins, are absolutely remarkable animals. Found only in New Zealand, they are as 'kiwi' as the kiwi. They are rare, fascinating and beautiful.

In 1982, when we first became interested in these small dolphins, there were six scientific papers describing their coloration, size, shape and distribution. They contained only snippets about NZ dolphin biology, and almost nothing about their behaviour. In 1978, Dr Alan Baker published a thorough summary of everything known about NZ dolphin. It was four pages long.

To redress this lack of information, we set out on a detailed study in 1984. Starting with the most obvious question of 'where are they and how many are there?', we surveyed every coastal area in which NZ dolphins were regularly seen, covering about 4500 nautical miles (8300 km) in a 3.9 m inflatable boat over six months. That survey provided not only an adventure with a few mildly terrifying moments, but also the first reliable data on the distribution of NZ dolphins. Eventually, we repeated this survey with a team of five observers, using binoculars, on a 15 m sailing catamaran. (We sold our house to buy the boat.)

From 1985 to 1989, we lived in Wainui (in the one-room Wainui School, which was unused for lack of pupils), on the shores of Akaroa Harbour on Banks Peninsula. We each had areas of specialty: Liz on the dolphins' behaviour and breeding, Steve on the sounds they make and how they use them. Together we identified the dolphins by photographing those with distinctive nicks or scars. We also put the word out that we would like to examine any dolphins killed in fishing gear or found dead on beaches. We wanted to learn what these dolphins ate, how fast they grew, when they reached sexual maturity and how long they lived.

The number of dead dolphins we received came as a massive surprise. As a result, the focus of some of our work shifted to how many were being caught by fishers and whether that was sustainable.

This research led to the creation of New Zealand's first Marine Mammal Sanctuary, and later to a comprehensive package of protected areas for NZ dolphins. Almost all of the information resulting from our studies is published in scientific journals, but they are not always easy to get hold of, and scientific papers are usually not easy to read – even for a scientist.

So that's where this book fits in. We will let you into some of the dolphins' secrets and bring you up to date with the latest research results. The book is intended for readers of all ages. It includes information that would fit neatly into a school project as well as in-depth information for university students and other interested readers. It is written for people seriously interested in biology, as well as for those simply captivated by dolphins.

Dolphins jump for social reasons, and also to have a look around.

WHAT'S IN A NAME?

THE NEW ZEALAND dolphin was scientifically described in 1881 by Belgian fossil expert P.J. van Beneden. Following the scientific, two-name system used to classify all plants and animals, the official name for the species is *Cephalorhynchus hectori.* Since the first name of any species is the name for the genus or group of species to which it belongs, *Cephalorhynchus* is a group of four dolphin species, which includes NZ dolphin, Chilean dolphin and two other species living off the coasts of Argentina and South Africa respectively.

The name *Cephalorhynchus* comes from the Greek words *kephalos* (head) and *rhynchos* (beak) and describes the way the whole head looks like a broad beak. The second part of the official name for the NZ dolphin is *hectori,* in honour of Sir James Hector who examined the first scientific specimen. Hector was the first director of the Colonial Museum (now known as the Museum of New Zealand Te Papa Tongarewa) and was without doubt the country's most influential scientist when he retired in 1903.

The dolphin is most frequently known as Hector's dolphin. Internationally, and in New Zealand, there is a trend away from such names. That the species was named after Sir James Hector is really relevant only to history buffs. It is better for a species' common name to reflect what it looks like, or where it is found. For this reason, Hooker's sea lion is now known as New Zealand sea lion. Likewise, NZ dolphin is a much better name than Hector's dolphin. After all, it is found only in New Zealand.

There are several Māori names for the species. The earliest included tutumairekurai, tūpoupou, pahu and popoto. Tutumairekurai is probably the most common, and means 'special ocean dweller'. Some Māori believed that the spirits of the dead would become tutumairekurai. Tūpoupou means to rise up vertically. Perhaps this name originated from the dolphin's habit of 'spyhopping'. Popoto is

WHICH DOLPHIN IS IT?

Of all dolphins in our waters, NZ dolphins are the easiest to identify as they have a rounded dorsal fin. The other species all have a triangular or sickle-shaped fin (see p. 7). So, if you see a dolphin with a rounded dorsal fin, you have seen a NZ dolphin. Of course, there are other cues to look for as well. NZ dolphins are very small and predominantly light grey. Adults are normally between 1.2 and 1.4 m long, and adult females are, on average, about 10 cm longer than males. Consequently, the males appear stockier; a very experienced observer can often tell adult males from females by body shape alone.

The four dolphin species common in New Zealand. Drawings are to scale.

Bottlenose dolphin.

Common dolphin.

Dusky dolphin.

NZ dolphin.

Photograph: Liz Slooten.

A mother and calf surfacing.

a commonly used name for NZ dolphin in the North Island and pahu is the South Island equivalent. The name pahu sounds like the exhalation of a NZ dolphin. Unfortunately, none of the Māori names remain in widespread use, perhaps because Māori in different regions had their own names for the species. There is no one name used by everyone.

There are at least four genetically distinct populations, one off the North Island and three off the South Island (east, west and south coasts). One of the genetic (mitochondrial DNA) haplotypes is found only off the North Island, which led to a 2002 proposal to call the North Island population a separate subspecies known as Maui's dolphin. Maui's dolphins are slightly larger (~10 cm) than the South Island subspecies, but look the same. There's no reliable way to tell them apart visually.

Despite being very familiar to coastal fishers, surfers and others using our coastal waters, NZ dolphins received very little public attention until the 1980s. Surprisingly few people knew they were endemic to this country. Some people called them 'puffing pigs' – surely as unglamorous a name as one could think of! Most folks simply, but mistakenly, called them porpoises.

NZ dolphins are true dolphins. They are members of the family *Delphinidae*, which includes 86 species worldwide. The NZ dolphin is the smallest member of the family, and the killer whale (orca – yes, it really is a dolphin!) is the largest. The NZ dolphin's lack of a bottle-shaped snout sometimes causes people to call them porpoises. However, true porpoises are members of the family *Phocoenidae*. Although it seems obscure, their most diagnostic feature is that they all have flattened, spade-shaped teeth, while dolphins have round, conical teeth. Dolphins and porpoises also differ in their behaviour. Porpoises are mostly shy; they avoid boats and are seldom acrobatic. Dolphins are much more demonstrative and spectacular. Only one porpoise (spectacled porpoise) has been seen in New Zealand waters, and only a very few times. Confusing dolphins with porpoises is not something you have to worry about.

Dolphin group bowriding our research boat. As well as getting an underwater view of what they are doing, we can use these pictures to see if a dolphin is female or male.

THE WHĀNAU (FAMILY)

THE ANCESTRY of whales and dolphins can be traced back to Pakicetus, a 53 million-year-old fossil found in Pakistan. Pakicetus was probably amphibious – a kind of transitional stage between land mammals and whales. Modern dolphins appeared on the scene relatively recently, at around 11 million years ago.

Although they are strikingly different in coloration, the four species in NZ dolphin's genus are very similar in habits and behaviour. All are small and typically found in shallow water close to shore. They are also Southern Hemisphere dolphins. NZ dolphin is found only in New Zealand; Heaviside's dolphin is found around the tip of South Africa and along the west coast to Namibia; and South America has two species. The Chilean dolphin is found in the inshore waters of Chile, while the striking black-and-white Commerson's dolphin has the most extensive distribution of the four *Cephalorhynchus* dolphin species. It is most common along the coasts of Argentina, Tierra del Fuego, and

Photograph: Simon Elwen.

Photograph: Marine Mammal Lab, SENPAT, Puerto Madryn, Chile.

Clockwise from top left: NZ dolphin, Chilean dolphin, Heaviside's dolphin and Commerson's dolphin.

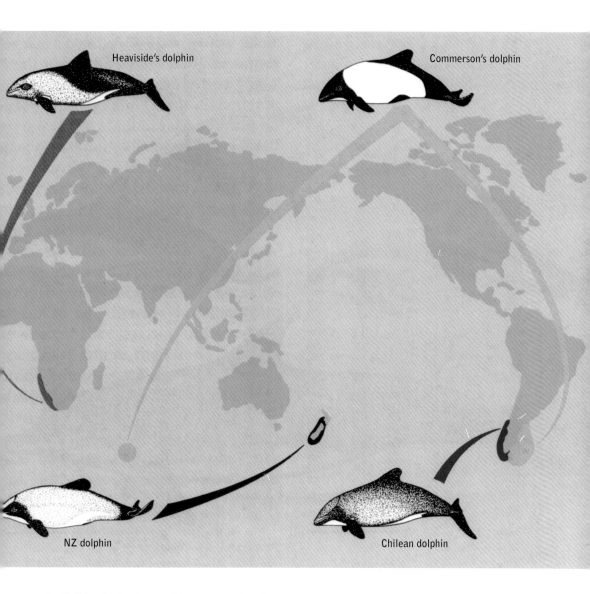

Heaviside's dolphin

Commerson's dolphin

NZ dolphin

Chilean dolphin

the Falkland Islands. In addition, an isolated population of Commerson's dolphin occurs about 8000 km away at the Kerguelen Islands in the Indian Ocean. These dolphins are larger than those in South America. They also retain their juvenile coloration (a grey haze over the white areas) into adulthood and have a different number of ribs attaching to the breastbone. These sorts of differences suggest that this population was founded by only a very few dolphins, perhaps as recently as a few tens of thousands of years ago.

DISTRIBUTION

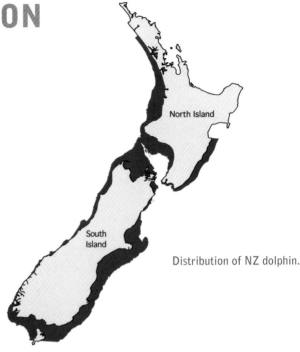

North Island

South
Island

Distribution of NZ dolphin.

NEW ZEALAND DOLPHINS are found close to shore almost everywhere around the South Island. They are shallow water animals. Sightings in waters more than 100 m deep are rare, which may explain why they are very seldom seen in the waters of Fiordland. Around the North Island, most recent sightings have been in the area between Cape Egmont and the Hokianga Harbour. NZ dolphins are also occasionally seen in Wellington Harbour and off the Kapiti and Wairarapa coasts, and were apparently much more frequently seen in these areas in the past.

Their distribution is patchy and fragmented, with small local resident populations. For example, on the south coast of the South Island, NZ dolphins are found mostly in Te Waewae Bay and Porpoise Bay, with a few sightings along the 130 km stretch of coast in between. Off the Otago coastline, you can find NZ dolphins near Moeraki and Karitane, in Blueskin Bay and around Taiaroa Head. But there is a gap in their distribution between Karitane and Moeraki. Population fragmentation has almost certainly been caused by a combination of small alongshore home ranges (individuals typically range along less than 50 km of coastline) and human impacts that are not evenly spread around the coastline. In several places (for example Taranaki), high levels of gillnet bycatch, now and in the past, have removed dolphins from the area or reduced local populations to very low levels. The genetics of NZ dolphins reflect this,

The NZ dolphin is a shallow water animal, usually found close to shore.

with differences between the populations of the south, east and west coasts of the South Island. Even within these regions, there are small, cumulative differences between each adjacent population that add up to a relatively large genetic difference between NZ dolphins at the top and bottom of the South Island east coast, for example. Photographic identification data back this up as well. Evidence from a large amount of photo-ID work around the South Island and off the North Island west coast shows that the longest distance over which individual NZ dolphins are known to travel is just over 100 km.

The total population has been estimated at 7270 NZ dolphins around the South Island and at 55 (individuals one year or older) off the North Island west coast. The very small populations on the north and south coasts of the South Island and off the North Island west coast are at greatest risk. Population fragmentation means that there is very little chance for a dolphin that dies (from natural causes or human impacts) to be replaced by a dolphin from a neighbouring population. Therefore, the fragmented distribution makes the dolphins' future much less secure. Small populations are much less resilient both to human impact and to environmental changes and catastrophes such as severe storms, toxic algal blooms and disease.

NZ dolphin is the most coastal dolphin species found in New Zealand waters. On open coasts they are often seen surfing or just beyond the surf line, and sometimes they will surf into water that is less than a metre deep. Akaroa Harbour is the best place to see NZ dolphins; it is truly a world-class place to go dolphin watching. Up to 100+ NZ dolphins can be in the harbour at any one time. On a calm summer's day, it is very unusual not to see them in Akaroa Harbour.

Everywhere these dolphins have been studied, more are seen close inshore in summer than in winter. This change is greatest at Banks Peninsula. In summer, about 80 per cent of the population is within 4 nautical miles of the shore (7.4 km). The distribution is more evenly spread in winter, with about half as many dolphins close to shore. In winter they also spend less time in harbours. Several of their prey species come inshore in spring and summer to spawn, and it is likely that the dolphins are following them inshore.

Being so small, NZ dolphins probably find it difficult to feed on the bottom in deep water. Banks Peninsula has a broad expanse of gently shelving shallow water to the north and south, formed by sediment from the Waimakariri and Rakaia rivers, and so offers a vast area within the diving range of NZ dolphins. The much steeper gradient of the South Island west coast offers a much narrower strip of foraging depths. We think this is why the dolphins range to 20 nautical miles off Banks Peninsula but only 6 nautical miles off the west coast, and why the seasonal change in distribution is much less obvious on the west coast.

There is no evidence that NZ dolphins migrate. For example, at Banks Peninsula we see the same identified dolphins year round. At Banks Peninsula we have studied these seasonal changes in distribution in detail, including how the dolphins' use of

Akaroa Harbour changes between summer and winter. We placed T-PODs (acoustic data loggers) in three different places in the harbour, to study how much time the dolphins spent in the inner, mid and outer harbour. We found that in the outer harbour, near the harbour entrance, dolphins were present year-round, with very little difference between summer and winter. In the mid-harbour, near Onuku, there was a noticeable seasonal pattern, with dolphins more common in summer than winter. This seasonal pattern was most obvious in the inner harbour, near Duvauchelle, where NZ dolphins were much more common in summer than in winter. However, they were still present on 41 per cent of the days on which recreational fishers are allowed to use gillnets (1 April to 1 November). This compromise to the dolphin protection regulations was put in place because visual surveys suggested that the dolphins rarely use this part of the harbour in winter. However, the new data from acoustic surveys shows that it is not safe to use gillnets in Akaroa Harbour at any time of year.

We also tested for patterns of dolphin presence in relation to the time of day and stage of tide. NZ dolphins were more common in the inner harbour in the early morning and more common in the outer harbour in the evening and at night. There were no clear patterns relating to the tides, which was a surprise.

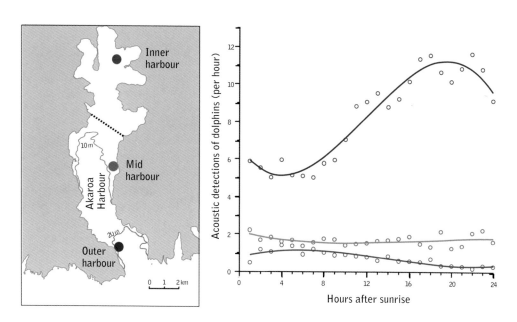

Above: Akaroa Harbour. Right: Acoustic recorders show how NZ dolphins use Akaroa Harbour at different times of day. Coloured dots on the map relate to the curves of acoustic detections.

HOW DO YOU COUNT DOLPHINS?

Liz measuring the distance to a dolphin group, using an inclinometer, on one of the aerial surveys.

IT IS RELATIVELY easy to count NZ dolphins because they are typically found in small groups. It is rare to see groups of more than 20, and the most common group size is 2–10 individuals. But estimating the size of a dolphin population involves much more than simply counting them.

The most recent survey of NZ dolphins (1996–2004) was a 'line-transect' survey. Worldwide, this is considered 'best practice' for dolphin surveys. Before undertaking our own surveys, we first joined leading scientists from the US National Marine Fisheries Service (NMFS) in line-transect surveys for marine mammals off the coast of the USA and Mexico. Then we invited Dr Paul Wade, a survey expert from NMFS, to help us get started with the first NZ dolphin survey.

On a line-transect survey from a boat, the observers scan the water in front and to the side with binoculars and with the naked eye, and measure the distance to each sighting. As you would expect, the observers see nearly all of the dolphins close to the boat, and the proportion they miss increases with distance from the boat. A dolphin surfacing more than a kilometre away is unlikely to be seen at all.

Next, you make a graph of the number of sightings at different distances from the trackline of the boat or plane you're using for the survey. This is used to estimate dolphin density (the number of dolphins per square kilometre). But it is not enough by itself. You also need to estimate the 'fraction missed' – which you can do by tracking sightings from a helicopter and scoring whether or not the boat-based observers saw them. This also helps determine whether a correction is needed for 'responsive movement' – that is, whether the dolphins are attracted to the survey vessel or avoid it. If they are attracted to boats, as NZ dolphins are, the number of sightings made from the boat will over-estimate the number of dolphins in the area, and that needs to be corrected for.

Of course, you also need a survey design that covers the dolphins' distribution fairly. Once the density estimates are properly corrected for the fraction missed and responsive movement, you multiply them by the area of the dolphins' habitat to estimate total population size.

We also adapted these methods to work from a twin-engined aircraft. Aircraft have the advantage of covering ground much faster, and cause no responsive movement in the dolphins. The downside is that you see a much smaller proportion of the population, and that needs to be carefully accounted for.

Scientists usually refer to the number of individuals in a population as a population 'estimate'. This does not imply any guesswork. It simply acknowledges that for most animal populations, including humans, it is not possible to physically count every single individual alive at any one time. Using sophisticated statistical methods gets around this problem.

Observers on the viewing platform of *Catalyst*.

UNDERSTANDING BEHAVIOUR

BEHAVIOUR TOWARDS BOATS

You don't need detailed analysis to realise that NZ dolphins are strongly attracted to boats, especially those travelling relatively slowly (less than 10 knots). Typically you'll see several dolphins swimming fast towards the boat, making lots of spray as they surface, and perhaps jumping in long, low leaps. Though they ride the bow wave and jockey amongst themselves for the best position, they normally break off after a hundred metres or so. If the boat slows down, or turns back, they often return to the bow wave, or surf in the wake.

The dolphins' behaviour towards boats and humans depends very much on what they are doing before we come along. If they are busy feeding, it is unlikely they will take much interest. However, if not busy with something else, they can be very curious and sociable. They often associate with a drifting boat, coming back to visit briefly each time they surface from a dive. These are ideal conditions in which to watch their behaviour.

Bowriding seen from in the water.

Dolphins bowriding one of the dolphin-watching boats in Akaroa Harbour.

JUMPS

If you watch the dolphins long enough you'll see three kinds of jumps. The most common is vertical and sometimes very high, with nose-first re-entry and very little splash. These vertical jumps are usually not repeated several times in a row by the same dolphin, but sometimes they can be contagious; one dolphin jumping causes others to jump as well.

Horizontal jumps are long and low, and made while swimming at speed. Some dolphin species do this because travelling this way saves energy over a long distance. NZ dolphins, however, seldom swim fast for more than a few hundred metres; these jumps are most often seen when the dolphins are racing to the bow wave of a boat, or chasing one another.

Both vertical and horizontal jumps make little splash and, therefore, little underwater noise. Making as *much* splash as possible seems to be the aim of a third type of jump. These noisy leaps are usually repeated many times, the dolphin slapping back into the water on its side or front. We have seen dolphins jump 20 times in a row this way, each jump being a little less high than the last, as the dolphin gets tired.

These different leaps often follow one another and seem to indicate excitement. They frequently occur in sexual or aggressive contexts, and sometimes seem to be just for fun. Vertical jumps are especially common in play-chases and after a particularly good ride when the dolphins are surfing. Sometimes vertical jumps seem to be used simply to have a look around. Noisy jumps seem to be attention-getters, a noisy signal most often made in highly social contexts.

Lots of jumping in NZ dolphins indicates a high level of social excitement. Most frequently this happens when two or more small groups come together to form an active bunch of 12–20 individuals. These larger groups are very temporary, usually splitting up again within 30 minutes. Chasing is very common, and there may be lots of body contact, which can be very gentle or quite forceful.

This photo sequence shows a dolphin doing a 'side flop', first hurling itself out of the water and then

Above, clockwise from left: Vertical jump and horizontal jump. Sometimes two or more dolphins jump at the same time.

splashing back down on its side.

LOBTAILING

After jumps, the most obvious behaviour in this very active state is called 'lobtailing'. This involves the dolphin hitting the water surface with its tail, usually many times in a row. This seems to be another attention-getting signal, and is most often done upside down – which makes sense, if making a loud noise is the aim.

The muscles of the back lie both above the spine and below it. The ones above (*longissimus dorsi*) move the tail up, while the ones below (*hypaxialis lumborum*) move the tail down. But the muscles above the spine are larger by far, so the real power stroke in swimming is the up-stroke. Since the up-stroke is more powerful, it is not surprising that when the dolphins want to hit the water as hard as possible, they do so upside down. When a dolphin both swims and lobtails upside down, it is easy for us to see if a particular dolphin is male or female.

Dolphins (and whales) lobtail by forcefully hitting the water surface with their tail. This can be done while swimming upside down (opposite page and photo sequence 1–2) or normal way up (3–5) and is usually done several times. We have seen from two or three lobtails to more than 20 done in quick succession by the same dolphin.

SEX

As far as we know, no species of dolphin or whale is monogamous (having one partner for life). Indeed, dolphins almost define the other end of the spectrum, as they have many sexual partners. Sexual behaviour is common and is often a group activity with several dolphins involved. Copulation takes only a few seconds and may be repeated many times in a few minutes. The weightless environment provides such a variety of positions that there is no characteristic way they 'do it'. Sex usually occurs in highly social groups showing most of the boisterous behaviours already described.

Some of the sexual signalling is very obvious. For example, an excited male often shows his penis, which is normally retracted into his genital slit to aid streamlining. Both males and females show sexual interest by presenting their belly towards another. As the genital slits of males and females have a different colour pattern, this is also a powerful visual signal. Often males and females alternately 'flash' at each other this way.

When interested in sex, male dolphins can be quite insistent, and sometimes we see clear indications that a particular female is *not* interested. Most frequently she does the opposite of the 'belly present', and simply turns on her side, her genital slit facing away from the male. She may also swim at the surface upside down, so that males cannot get access. Occasionally one or more males will chase a female vigorously, attempting to copulate with her, usually with lots of fast swimming, very tight turns, and sometimes horizontal jumps. Sometimes one male will 'pounce' on a female, making contact with his chest or belly.

Copulation can be seen at any time of year, but is more common in the breeding season (late summer to autumn).

Gentle body contact between a female (at the top of the photo) and a male.

The 'pounce' is included in the social/sexual behaviour category. It is done either while swimming slowly (photo sequence 1, 2, 3) or faster and more forcefully (4). Aggressive behaviour is rarely seen in NZ dolphins, but this female and calf were chased around for several minutes by other individuals (5).

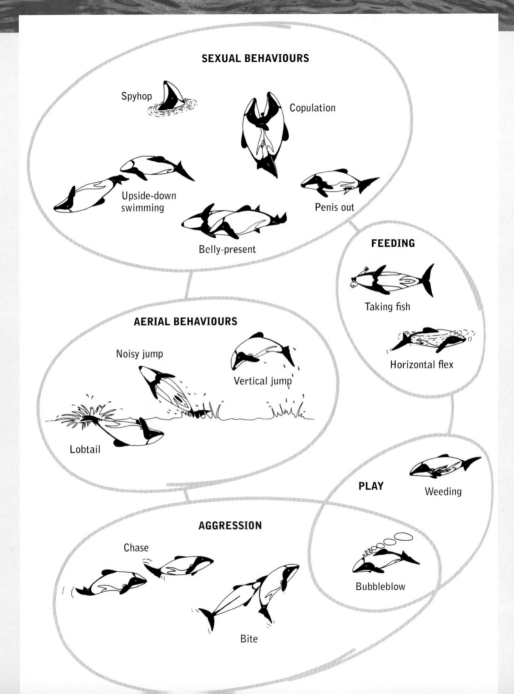

SEXUAL BEHAVIOURS

Spyhop

Copulation

Upside-down swimming

Penis out

Belly-present

FEEDING

Taking fish

Horizontal flex

AERIAL BEHAVIOURS

Noisy jump

Vertical jump

Lobtail

PLAY

Weeding

Bubbleblow

AGGRESSION

Chase

Bite

UNDERSTAND THE BEHAVIOUR OF ANOTHER SPECIES?

WITHOUT BEING ABLE to ask dolphins why they do things, can we do better than guess? Some behaviours are easy to interpret; for example, copulation is by definition a sexual behaviour, and one dolphin biting another is obviously aggressive. Most behaviours are harder to figure out. Researchers usually assign meanings that they think are sensible, but different researchers interpret behaviours differently, and the real meaning of the behaviour (to the dolphin) can be lost in the confusion.

One powerful clue about the meaning of behaviours is the order in which the dolphins use them. A behaviour that typically occurs soon after, or just before, another probably has a related meaning. By watching groups of dolphins and noting the times particular behaviours occur, then recording which behaviours follow, we can come a step closer to figuring out what these behaviours mean.

This process uses a statistical method called sequence analysis. This shows which behaviours are associated more strongly than we would expect by chance. Next, we draw a diagram with behaviours shown close together if they tend to follow each other. By checking the position of a particular behaviour relative to behaviours whose meaning is clear, we can judge what each behaviour means and see how they are related. You could say that this process lets the dolphins tell us what their behaviour means. This forms the basis of our understanding of NZ dolphin behaviour.

Opposite page: Behaviour sequence analysis revealed the behaviour categories shown in this diagram. For example, upside-down swimming and belly-presenting seem to have something to do with sexual behaviour. Jumps and lobtails indicate excitement and can be associated with either sexual or aggressive behaviour.

Trudi Webster and Will Rayment used a polecam to find out that small groups of NZ dolphins tend to be either all male or all female, while larger groups tend to be mixed.

Dolphins herding a tight 'ball' of sprats against the water surface, and taking turns feeding – with gulls getting in on the action from above.

Below: Barracuda eat the same small fish the dolphins feed on.

FEEDING

Like most wild animals, NZ dolphins spend a lot of their time feeding. When feeding at or near the bottom, they make dives of up to two minutes, then spend a minute or so at the surface, usually breathing 5–8 times before diving again. This routine can be kept up for hours. Feeding at the surface is less common but far more obvious, because you can often see the entire chase. The most common prey chased at the surface are sprats and yellow-eyed mullet.

Spyhopping, common during surface feeding, is also used in social situations.

Along with obvious chasing, two distinctive feeding behaviours are often seen. Commonly, the chasing dolphin will poke its chin or head out of the water and turn on its vertical axis – as if this were a faster way to turn. This behaviour is called 'spyhopping'. The dolphin comes far enough out of the water to get a good look at what is going on above the surface. In the other odd feeding behaviour, the horizontal flex, the dolphin stops dead at the surface, and hunches its back two or three times. Occasionally we have seen them catching tiny fish while they're doing this.

Surface feeding often involves several dolphins, usually taking only one small fish at a time. Sometimes it looks more like the dolphins are playing rather than feeding seriously. Seabirds, especially white-fronted terns, are often attracted to the dolphins when they are feeding near the surface, and sometimes dive into the water very close to the dolphins and catch fish scared up by the activity. We have rarely seen NZ dolphins working a tight 'ball' of fish at the surface, as other dolphins (and tuna and swordfish) do. It is a spectacular sight when it happens.

NZ dolphins often play
with bits of seaweed
(above and below) and
occasionally with sticks
and other flotsam. Here
one tries to balance a
leaf on its snout (right).

PLAY

One of the reasons why dolphins capture our imagination is that they do many things apparently just for fun: they 'play'. Play is very common in young mammals, but tends to disappear in adults. Perhaps because we humans enjoy 'play' throughout our lives, we regard it as a sign of intelligence. Certainly, dolphins of all ages spend a lot of time playing.

Surfing is very common at beaches such as Porpoise Bay in Southland, on the South Island west coast, and in rough weather anywhere. It often seems that when we are taking a fair beating in our boat, the dolphins are just starting to enjoy themselves! In calmer weather, playing with bits of weed is a favourite activity. By twisting just at the right moment, a dolphin can pick up a drifting piece of seaweed on its dorsal fin, flipper or tail flukes. They will carry it there for a few seconds until it falls off or until another dolphin 'steals' it. These seaweed games are usually short, but are very common. Occasionally dolphins play with floating sticks and leaves.

Underwater bubbleblows are a sign of building excitement within the group. These can be used in play and sexual behaviour, but also in aggression. Our best explanation is that they simply signal excitement, in much the same way that shouting does in humans: we shout when we are happy, afraid, aggressive, or just trying to get someone's attention.

Bubbleblows indicate excitement, and can be associated with play or aggression.

Photograph: Steve Bradley.

Aggression is rare
in NZ dolphins but,
as in all mammals,
it does occur.

AGGRESSION

Dolphins have a reputation for being remarkably non-aggressive with each other. In fact, this varies with different species, and all show aggression to some degree. Some species, for example bottlenose dolphins, can be quite aggressive. NZ dolphins, however, are reasonably benign. They certainly chase, bite and occasionally hit one another with their flukes, but these acts are momentary and seldom produce serious injury. We've never seen a 'fight', in the way that dogs fight, with both individuals repeatedly attacking each other. Normally, a dolphin that has just received a bite will simply swim away, rather than fight back.

Despite the low intensity of the aggression, almost all NZ dolphins bear marks from it. The outer layer of skin is constantly renewing itself; this is how dolphins avoid fouling by barnacles, bryozoans, algae, ascidians and other organisms. But it also means that the skin is soft and easily damaged – much more so than human skin. Toothrakes are the most common injury by far. They are shallow, parallel cuts that look like they were made by the sharp points of a wide fork dragged across the skin. Toothrakes usually heal within a few weeks without leaving a lasting scar. NZ dolphins are not aggressive towards people.

A bite from another
dolphin leaves
a characteristic
toothrake mark
(left).

33

FRIENDS AND RELATIVES

BECAUSE NZ DOLPHINS are usually seen in small groups, it is tempting to think these are families: Mum, Dad, and the kids. Although human groups often work that way (also those of many birds), 'nuclear' families are actually uncommon among mammals. A few dolphins and whales have very stable groups: for example, some killer whale (orca) groups are stable over decades, and 'nursery' groups of female and immature sperm whales are also very stable. Almost all other cetaceans (the collective term for whales, dolphins and porpoises) have unstable groups; we seldom see the same individuals consistently hanging around together.

However, females and their offspring are the basis of all mammalian social systems, because the females feed (and educate) their young. Dolphin calves depend on milk for only the first six months or so, but may suckle occasionally for much longer. Mums and calves typically stay together for at least two years. During this time the calf undoubtedly

A typical small group of NZ dolphins. Opposite page: Dolphins surfacing in Akaroa Harbour on a calm morning.

Several dolphins jumping out of the water at the same time usually indicates a very active group.

learns a lot from its mother about finding food, the dos and don'ts of social interactions, how to deal with predators and how to use their sophisticated sonar system.

Associations between other individuals are weak. The 'fission-fusion' nature of groups is very easy to see if you watch NZ dolphins for a few hours, because the small groups come together, intermingle, then split again. The new groups are often quite different, having gained, lost, or swapped members. But, while groups are unstable and only mums and calves are *always* seen together, individuals do have 'best friends' with whom they are seen more often.

Though NZ dolphins spend most of their time in small groups, what happens when those groups come together is very important. It is in these temporary larger groups that most social behaviour occurs. Sometimes several dolphins jump or lobtail at once, chase each other, or sprint for short distances to suddenly turn and race back to the main action. In the midst of this there is a lot of more subtle signalling.

Behaviours associated with sex are much more common after two groups have just joined, as if they are excited to see one another. This observation has implications for conservation: dolphins in low population areas may breed more slowly than those in more populous areas. Where groups come in contact less often, less sex results in lower pregnancy rates.

SOUNDS AND COMMUNICATION

UNDER WATER, vision is a very limited sense. In very clear water we can see perhaps 50 m; in air we would consider this a dense fog. Because water carries sound very well – almost five times faster than air – sound is the obvious way to transmit information under water.

In contrast with most other dolphins, almost all of the sounds produced by NZ dolphins are very short (1/7000 second), high-frequency clicks centred on 120 kHz, about six times higher than we can hear. Most clicks have a very narrow band of frequencies and are made up of a single pulse, but some have

two or three pulses within one click. Clicks are emitted in sequences of a few dozen to several thousand, depending on what the dolphin is doing. A simple question, such as 'how far away is that boat?', may require only a few clicks. However, finding a fish, determining its range, speed, direction, size and species, then chasing it down while it tries to outmanoeuvre its predator, may take thousands of clicks.

When dolphins are echolocating, clicks are emitted so that outgoing clicks and returning echoes don't overlap. Because of this, and to maximise the information from echoes,

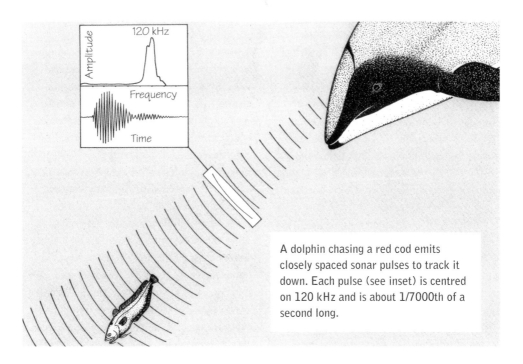

A dolphin chasing a red cod emits closely spaced sonar pulses to track it down. Each pulse (see inset) is centred on 120 kHz and is about 1/7000th of a second long.

dolphins click faster as they get closer to the target. In the final approach, the dolphin may emit several hundred clicks each second.

NZ dolphins make very few sounds that are audible to humans. They do not whistle as other dolphins do, but some of their loudest clicks have low frequencies that are audible. Sometimes, especially when a group is very active socially, a squeal or crying sound is heard. These are very strange sounds, made up of high-frequency clicks repeated at such a high rate that the repetition rate is audible, while the clicks are not. Once the click rate rises above about 200 clicks per second, it is audible as a tone. Thus, when a dolphin makes high-frequency clicks 500 times per second, we hear a tone of 500Hz – even though the individual clicks are far beyond our hearing. The highest click rate yet recorded from a NZ dolphin is 1149 clicks per second, one of the highest rates recorded from any dolphin.

The maximum sound pressure recorded from NZ dolphins is 163dB.* This is equivalent to 101dB in air – a bit less than a loud rock concert. In comparison, bottlenose dolphins can produce clicks at 220dB (roughly 158dB in air, and louder than a 747 airliner on takeoff). The decibel (dB) scale is logarithmic, so these very loud bottlenose dolphin clicks contain about half a million times more energy than those of NZ dolphins. Even though bottlenose clicks are extraordinarily loud, they are not loud enough to stun prey before capture – as the now-rejected 'big bang' hypothesis suggested.

For many years, researchers have assumed that dolphins communicate with their low-frequency sounds (such as whistles) and echolocate with their high-frequency clicks. While this is certainly true, it does not mean that clicks are used solely for echolocation. The best evidence for this is from NZ dolphins, which use certain types of high-frequency clicks predominantly when in large groups and in social interactions.

It is clear that NZ dolphins (like other dolphins) do not use anything like human language. Human language involves *symbolism* – using sounds as symbols for particular objects or actions, and *syntax* – the idea that meaning depends on the order in which symbols occur (for example, *dog bites man* does not mean the same as *man bites dog*). Dolphins do not appear to use anything like a vocabulary of symbols, and there is no evidence that the order of the sounds is important. None of this means that dolphins are incapable of sophisticated communication, it simply means that it is not useful to compare it to human language. Humans have so far failed to decipher dolphin communication – or indeed the language of any other mammal.

Dolphins have an echolocation system of exquisite sophistication – far, far beyond the most advanced human-made sonar systems. In addition, dolphins use signals to indicate emotional state (whistles in many species, cries in NZ dolphins), and there is good evidence that different sounds are used in different social contexts. There is also evidence suggesting that dolphins do not need perfect knowledge of the outgoing sonar signal to make sense of the incoming echoes. This means that other dolphins can tell what an echolocating dolphin is looking at, where it is, and what it is doing. Because echolocation is a

---

*   the reference level for this measurement is 1μPa at 1m.

three-dimensional sense, dolphins can almost certainly use their sonar to tell if one among them is pregnant (pregnant human mothers frequently have ultrasound scans to check on the baby), fed recently, or is frightened. Sounds indicating emotional state fill out the picture. Think about it: if you knew precisely what others around you were doing and feeling, how much would you need to talk to them?

This idea, called the 'eavesdropping hypothesis', was proposed with NZ dolphins in mind. There is some support from the wild (it is hard to test the idea convincingly with wild dolphins), and studies with captive bottlenose dolphins have provided strong evidence that silent dolphins can extract information about objects by listening to the echoes generated by the sonar activity of others.

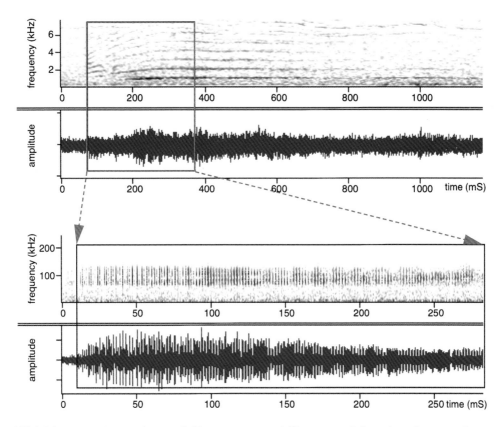

NZ dolphins sometimes make sounds like a cry or squeal. The top panel shows how these sound to the human ear. The enlarged area shows that this sound is actually made up of high-frequency clicks made so fast that the repetition rate (~1000 clicks/sec) is audible as a tone of ~1000 Hz. The equally spaced lines above that are harmonics.

HOW DO DOLPHINS MAKE

ALTHOUGH THE SOUNDS made by NZ dolphins have been studied in detail, *how* they are made has not been studied. For clues we must look to studies of other dolphins in which this question has received a lot of attention. In the most detailed studies, dolphins and porpoises have been trained to vocalise while *inside* a medical CAT or MRI scanner or with an endoscope in their nasal airways.

Unlike other mammals, dolphins have a larynx without vocal cords. This does not necessarily mean that the larynx is not involved in sound production at all (it seems to function mostly to regulate airflow) but it does suggest that something else is the principal sound source. In dolphin evolution, the nostrils have moved from the end of the snout to the top of the head, and fused to make one blowhole. Immediately below them is the vestibular sac – an air sac that acts to recycle the air used to make sounds, so that the dolphin does not need to release bubbles in order to vocalise. Below this, and above a further pair of air sacs that appear to work as reflectors to direct sound forwards, are two sets of 'phonic lips'. It is thought that when they relax slightly, letting a pulse of high-pressure air past, a high-frequency click is made.

The inside of a dolphin's head. The larynx, phonic lips, nasal air sacs and melon are all thought to be involved in making high-frequency clicks.

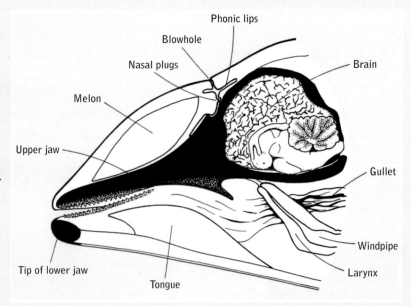

AND HEAR SOUNDS?

You can get a rough idea of how this might work by stretching the neck of an inflated balloon. Holding the neck at different tensions while releasing the air results in pulsed sounds of different frequencies. In the dolphin's head, once a click is made, it travels forwards through the melon, a body of waxy fat shaped like a flattened rugby ball in front of the dolphin's skull. The speed of sound changes within the melon, so sound is bent more at the edges than through the middle. In this way it works like a lens, focusing the clicks forward into a beam.

Though all dolphins have external ears, these are reduced to a tiny pinhole behind each eye. They are not functional: instead, dolphins hear with the lower jaw. This is known from an experiment with a blindfolded, captive dolphin trained to perform a task with its sonar system. Its lower jaw was covered by one of two identical-looking hoods, one which allowed sounds through, and one that did not. Both left the external ear uncovered. With the acoustically transparent hood in place, the dolphin could do the task easily. With the 'sound-proof' hood in place, it could not.

The sides of the lower jaw are very thin, and backed by fat very similar to that of the melon. The middle ear, which contains the structures that turn vibration into nerve impulses, is housed within a separate piece of bone on each side of the skull. Because these are free-floating – separate from the skull, and attached directly to the lower jaw – the dolphin can get directional hearing under water without being confused by sounds that are conducted through the skull.

Echolocation is the obvious way for dolphins to find their way around. Even in relatively clear water – rare in NZ dolphin habitat – vision is useful only at close ranges. The two dolphins close to the camera are clear, but the distant one is about four metres away and is already difficult to see.

DOLPHIN BIOLOGY

BEING MAMMALS, NZ dolphins breathe air, are warm-blooded and give birth to live young which suckle milk. They are also born with hair (a standard mammalian feature) but only a few (along the upper lip) and they are retained for only a few weeks after birth. Much of their basic anatomy is surprisingly similar to that of humans.

SKELETAL ANATOMY

Any dolphin skeleton shows the ancient terrestrial ancestry of its group. In the flipper, for example, are all the bones you have in your arm, wrist and fingers. They have telescoped and changed shape, and the finger bones have multiplied, but they are all there. All mammals, except sloths and manatees, have seven vertebrae in the neck. Dolphins also have seven, though in some species several have fused together. The most notable difference is the lack of a pelvis and hind limbs. Actually these are not entirely lost, but are reduced to two tiny bones that lie in the muscle where the pelvis 'should' be.

In length, the NZ dolphin is the smallest of all dolphins. It has only one competitor for the title of the smallest, depending on whether you choose smallest by length, or smallest by weight. The *franciscana*, which lives in South America's tropical estuaries and along the coast of Brazil, is a very lightly built dolphin whose very long and slender snout is a quarter of the dolphin's 1.5–1.7 m maximum length. A full-grown *franciscana* weighs about 10 kg less than a NZ dolphin. Adult female NZ dolphins reach just over 1.4 m (about 47 kg) and are about 10 cm longer and 10 kg heavier than adult males. This females-larger pattern is quite common among the smaller dolphins and porpoises. Interestingly, it is also the norm in the baleen whales: the largest animal that ever lived was a female blue whale.

This skeleton, drawn from one mounted in the Akaroa Museum, shows the unmistakable terrestrial ancestry of dolphins and their specialisation to an aquatic life. The bones of the shoulder and flipper are the same as in your shoulder, arm and hand, yet the small pair of bones (one on each side) floating underneath the spine is all that is left of the pelvis.

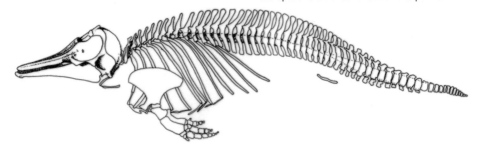

THE BRAINIEST DOLPHIN?

One of the reasons why dolphins and whales captivate our interest is that they have very large brains. The brain of an adult male sperm whale, at around 8 kg, is the largest on the planet, and makes our 1.2–1.3 kg brains look like walnuts. However, there's nothing particular about living in water that favours especially large brains. Dolphins and sharks are both successful predators at the top of the food chain, yet dolphins have brains that are 15–60 times larger than those of similarly sized sharks. A 38 kg adult NZ dolphin has a brain of around 640 g. Interestingly, this is one of the very highest brain weight to body weight ratios (1.7 per cent) known among dolphins, higher than that of any of the primates, and not far off the typical ratio for humans (1.9 per cent).

It is not known why dolphins have such large brains. Large brains are not essential for processing echoes in sophisticated echolocation. Bats perform similarly amazing feats of echolocation, yet most species have less than a gram of brain.

In addition to having very large brains, those parts of the brain associated with reasoning and creativity in humans are also large in dolphins. On the other hand, some features of the dolphin brain appear relatively primitive. Of course there are obvious differences, some of which relate to the way dolphins and humans experience their surroundings. Humans are predominantly visual animals, so the parts of our brains that process visual information are large. Dolphins rely far more on acoustic senses, and those parts of their brains are correspondingly large.

No one has a sensible answer to the question of just how intelligent dolphins are. Even if we could figure out exactly what intelligence is, making a fair comparison of the intelligence of two species that are so different is, so far, simply impossible.

KEEPING WARM

Water conducts heat much more effectively than air. In a 20°C bath, you would eventually die of exposure. Marine mammals must maintain a high body temperature (around 36–37°C), so insulation from cold is crucial. Seals solve the problem with two layers of fantastic fur, the inner layer so dense that the skin never gets wet. Dolphins and whales use blubber, a dense, oily, fat layer just under the skin, 2–3 cm thick in NZ dolphins and up to 50 cm thick in some whales. This provides insulation and acts as an energy store when food is hard to find. It is also the main reason why whales were so heavily hunted: their oil, boiled down from blubber, fuelled lamps and was used to make candles and margarine.

Within the blubber layer, whales and dolphins have a network of blood vessels that works like a heat exchanger. Heat is recovered from the vessels leading away from the heart by the interleaved vessels heading back to the heart. This is a clever way of recycling the heat, and reducing the amount that is lost to the outside environment.

NZ dolphins have two extra problems in conserving heat. They are found in water that is decidedly cool (down to 6°C at times!) Also, their very small size means that they have a relatively large surface area (high surface to volume ratio). That means more heat loss.

RAW FISH AGAIN?

The penalty of being warm-blooded is that it takes a lot of energy to sustain life. That is why cool-blooded reptiles take over in deserts, where food is scarce. In the early 1970s, four NZ dolphins were kept briefly at Napier's Marineland. An adult male, for which records are available, ate about 4 kg of fish daily (about 11 per cent of his body weight). Considering they eat so much, it is not surprising that in the wild NZ dolphins spend much of their time diving, apparently for food.

Most of what we know about diet is from sieving otoliths from the stomachs of dolphins killed in gillnets or found dead on beaches. Otoliths are the earbones of fish: small, dense bones not easily digested by stomach acid. Each fish species has otoliths of a diagnostic shape, so by sorting out these bones it is possible to figure out what fish were eaten. By measuring otoliths, we can even estimate what size fish they came from. From these studies it is clear that NZ dolphins feed on a wide variety of fish species, including bottom-dwelling species such as āhuru, red cod, stargazer and small flatfish. In mid-water and near the surface, small arrow squid, hake and hoki are taken when available. Sometimes they can be seen feeding right at the surface, chasing yellow-eyed mullet or sprats.

Rather than preferring certain species, it seems that NZ dolphins take whatever is around that is the right size. The largest prey items we have ever seen inside a NZ dolphin's stomach were a 44 cm (830 g) red cod and a 61 cm (960 g) arrow squid. Even with its tentacles folded up, that squid would have taken up all of the available room in the dolphin's stomach. At the other end of the scale, we've seen dolphins chasing individual whitebait!

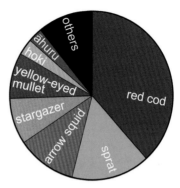

Male

Fish otoliths and squid beaks recovered from the stomachs of NZ dolphins (caught in fishing nets or found dead on a beach) are stored in small plastic bags – after careful cleaning.

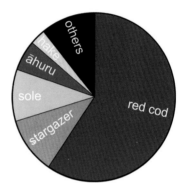

Female

The pie graphs above show that male dolphins eat a wider variety of prey than females.

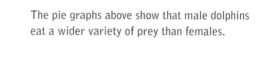

NZ dolphins eat surprisingly small prey. Most fish and squid they consume are smaller than 15 cm long. The horizontal axis indicates the size of the prey items, and the vertical axis shows the number of prey items recovered (from a total of 63 stomachs that were examined).

DIVING

No vertebrate animal can live without oxygen. Fish can absorb dissolved oxygen by passing water over their gills; diving mammals must take oxygen with them. Like human free-divers, they take some of it with them in their lungs, and some is held by the blood pigment haemoglobin. Seals carry extra oxygen with them by carrying extra blood, much more than a land mammal of similar size. But haemoglobin is not the only substance that can store oxygen. Myoglobin, found in unusually large quantities in the muscles of dolphins and whales, also stores oxygen, right where it is needed to sustain movement. The myoglobin in cetacean muscle is what makes it look so dark compared to the much redder muscle of other mammals.

Despite these features, NZ dolphins do not dive for very long. A good human free-diver can dive for the two minutes that NZ dolphins typically dive for, but cannot do it repeatedly as a dolphin can. After a few breaths at the surface over a minute or so, a NZ dolphin can dive again, and again – indeed they spend much of their time diving repeatedly like this. NZ dolphins do not seem to dive very deep. They are seen only rarely in water deeper than 100 m. Their diet includes fish that live on or near the bottom, so 80–100 m might be as far as they can dive and still have enough time to hunt.

Avoiding predators such as sharks and killer whales is often given as a reason for NZ dolphins preferring shallow water. This might be true elsewhere, but in New Zealand these predators are often seen in shallow coastal waters. The dolphins' preference for shallow water is related more to their feeding ecology. Their small size restricts their diving depth. Shallow inshore waters are generally more productive, with more potential prey, than deeper offshore waters. This is due primarily to the nutrient runoff from the land, and because coastal seaweeds, which are restricted to shallow water due to light penetration, contribute energy into the system by photosynthesis. So it makes sense for the dolphins to be where the most food is. Interestingly, in areas where the water is relatively shallow (for example, Banks Peninsula and other parts of the east coast of the South Island) NZ dolphins range much further offshore. Basically, wherever these dolphins are found, the 100 m depth contour provides a reasonable limit to their offshore range (red area in the map on p. 12).

THE NAUGHTY BITS

NZ dolphins, like all other whales and dolphins, have their sexual organs tucked away neatly in a genital slit. In females, the genital slit and anus are close together and look like one continuous slit, flanked on each side by small mammary slits from which their calves suckle. Not having lips as we do, calves cannot suck on a nipple. Instead, the mother has a layer of muscle over each of her mammary glands and, when prodded by the calf, literally squirts milk into the youngster's mouth. Calves have a feathery-tipped tongue, which may help get a better seal. The milk itself is extraordinarily rich. It needs to be; calves need fuel to keep their own temperature high, and need to grow fast to avoid predators.

NZ dolphins are colour-coded. Females have little if any grey around their genital slit, while on males the genital slit is further forward and has a distinctive grey oval around it.

Once you know what to look for, dolphins are easy to sex. In males the genital slit is much further forward from the anus, and there are no mammary slits. Male NZ dolphins make it even easier by having a dark grey patch around the genital slit. Females have a much smaller grey patch, or none at all. Except during sexual play, a male's penis, a strangely conical organ with a slight corkscrew, is kept withdrawn inside the slit. His testes are also inside, and are very large by comparison to most mammals. An adult NZ dolphin weighing 40 kg might easily have testes totalling 1.2 kg! That would be like an average human male having testes about twice as large as his brain. There are two reasons for this. First, NZ dolphins are promiscuous, copulating repeatedly in the breeding season, so they need lots of sperm. Second, sperm production is not so efficient at high temperatures. Having testes inside the body means you need bigger ones to do the same job.

REPRODUCTION

LIKE HUMANS, NZ dolphins do not have sex just for reproduction, but sex is most common when females are 'coming into season' or ovulating. The basics of reproduction in dolphins are similar to other mammals. The female's egg emerges from one of her ovaries (usually the left one; the right one is often inactive, as if it were a back up), into the uterus. If she mates with a male at this time, his sperm will swim towards the egg and try to fertilise it.

If this is successful, the fertilised egg implants in the wall of the uterus and begins to grow. As in other mammals, the growing calf is fed by its umbilical cord. The sac-like follicle in the ovary from which the egg was released turns into a gland, secreting hormones to maintain a pregnancy if the egg is fertilised. This gland is called a *corpus luteum*. If the egg is not fertilised, or after the pregnancy is over, this gland shrinks into a small, white, warty-looking *corpus albicans*, which permanently scars the ovary. These structures are very important, because when we examine a female dolphin found dead on a beach or in a net, that's how we can be sure that she was old enough to breed.

We can also tell if she has been pregnant. At birth, NZ dolphins weigh 8–10 kg, and are 60–75 cm long. They are very large compared to the size of their mothers, and the mother's uterus must stretch accordingly. Considering this, it is not surprising that even years after a female has given birth, her womb has very obvious stretch marks.

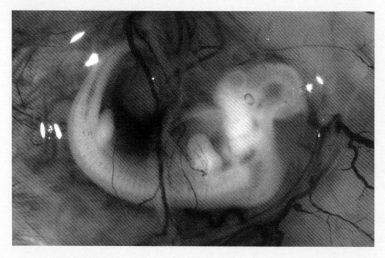

We found this foetus, estimated to be around six weeks old, in a female that had been killed in a gillnet. The hind limb buds develop not into pelvis and legs as they would in a land mammal, but into two small bones which 'float' in the muscle on either side of the backbone.

A very young calf, most likely just a day or so old, with the fold marks still showing as 'dents'.

BIRTH AND AGE

Despite the large size of the calf, dolphin births are generally quick and relatively easy – mostly because there is no bony pelvis in the way. Even after thousands of hours watching NZ dolphins, we have not yet been lucky enough to see a birth, but we have seen NZ dolphin calves very soon after birth.

The dorsal fin of a calf that is only a few hours old is still partly folded over. The overall coloration is darker, as if there is a dark tinge over the top of the normal (adult) coloration pattern. Mothers with newborn calves are usually much less interested in boats and only occasionally approach to bowride, but a

quick look on our part is usually enough to tell whether a calf is newborn or last year's. Newborns have a series of 4–6 vertical light grey stripes on their flanks. These 'fetal folds' are caused when the calf is curled up sideways in the womb. The skin forms creases, which disrupt the normal pigment pattern. Just as an unborn human baby kicks, the unborn calf flexes from side to side, so the fold marks show on both sides. These marks disappear as the darker grey of the calf fades to the adult hue, and by six months are invisible or nearly so.

Though studying living dolphins is much more pleasant, we have learnt a lot from

On this young dolphin, several weeks old, the fetal fold marks are still visible as lighter-coloured lines on the skin.

examining ones killed in fishing nets or found dead on beaches. Early on in the study, this is how we found out when dolphins start breeding and how long they live. Now that the photo-ID study has been going for more than a full lifespan of a NZ dolphin (nearly 30 years) we are starting to gather data on things like lifespan and reproductive rate from live dolphins.

We have performed autopsies on more than 120 NZ dolphins. Their age can be determined by examining their teeth. This work has shown that females have their first calf between seven and nine years old, and males reach sexual maturity around the same age, between six and nine years. The lifespan of NZ dolphins, based on the age of dead dolphins and observation of wild dolphins, is around 25 years. As with humans, only a very small proportion of the dolphins make it to the maximum age; only about 1 per cent make it to 25 years of age.

It is not possible to determine the age of free-swimming dolphins, but you can measure them and determine whether particular individuals are juveniles or mature. Trudi Webster used a laser system to measure NZ dolphins and figure out which individuals were up to six years old – which is when they stop growing – and which were older than six. This is very useful in determining how many mature individuals are in the population, and therefore the potential population growth rate.

While studies of dead dolphins can tell us whether a particular dolphin has ever had a calf, they cannot tell us how many she has had. The only foolproof way to discover that is to follow distinctive females over many years. Since 1984 we have built up a catalogue of individually distinctive dolphins at Banks Peninsula, which includes more than 100 mature females. By noting who has a calf and when, we have found that females breed, on average, every 2–4 years. By any standards, this is a very slow rate. If she lives to maximum age, a female NZ dolphin could be expected to have up to 5–8 calves. Almost all other mammals can reproduce much faster, but other dolphin species have a similarly low output. Understanding this, it becomes easy to see why dolphin populations are so vulnerable to human impacts.

HOW FAST CAN POPULATIONS GROW?

To figure out how fast NZ dolphins can breed we first need to estimate survival and reproductive rates. This can be done using photographic identification (see pp. 56–62). Every year, we analyse photographs to find out which individuals we have seen, which ones have bred, and which are 'missing in action'. 'Mark-recapture' statistical analysis of these records allows us to estimate survival rate – the probability of surviving from one year to the next.

We can then put the survival rate and reproductive rate into a population model to find out if the population is going up or down. It is a bit like accounting. We estimate the number of individuals added to the population each year (births) and the number removed (deaths) in order to find out if the population is growing, declining or stable. Most population models include only females. One male can fertilise several females, so if there were fewer males the population would still be fine. On the other hand, even a small reduction in the number of breeding females can cause a major decline in population size. To build a population model, we need to know when females start breeding, how long they live, how often they breed, and the proportion of females that survive each year. Some of this information comes from examining dead dolphins, but most of it comes from resighting individually distinctive dolphins over many years.

These calculations show that NZ dolphins have a maximum population growth of about 2 per cent per year. That is, without human impact, a population of 100 can grow at most to 102 the next year. This is only just enough insurance against prey shortages, disease, toxic plankton blooms and so on. In a 'bad' year, with rough weather conditions or poor availability of the fish and squid species the dolphins like to eat, the population may not grow at all. This low figure means that even very small numbers killed, for example in fishing gear, can easily cause populations to decline. Unless such impacts are controlled, they may cause extinction.

HOW CAN YOU TELL HOW OLD A DOLPHIN IS?

BEING ABLE to tell if a dead female dolphin was mature, or had been pregnant, is not very useful unless we can also tell how old she was. Unlike us, dolphins have only one set of teeth throughout their lives. Each tooth starts as a hollow cone, and each year two zones of dentine are deposited on the inside. After preparation of the tooth, these are visible as a wide, dark zone for each summer and a narrow, light zone for each winter. By counting the layers we can easily tell how old any dolphin was, a bit like reading the rings on a tree.

How do we prepare the tooth? To see the rings, the tooth first has to be decalcified. The hard calcium can be removed by soaking the tooth in acid for up to two days, by which time it has about the consistency of a raw carrot. Next, the tooth goes through a sequence of chemical baths so that any water is removed. It is then embedded in wax and the wax block is mounted on a microtome, which cuts slices only 2–4 thousandths of a millimetre thick. The final step is to stain the slices to make the layers more obvious. Then the tooth is examined under a microscope. To make sure the growth layers are counted accurately, each tooth section is double checked by someone else who doesn't know what the first reading was.

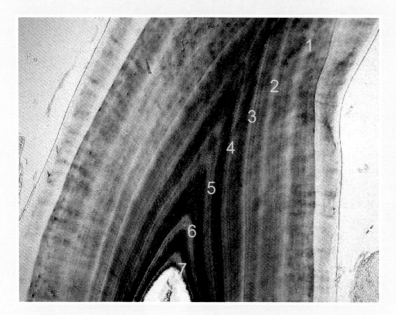

Layers of dentine are continuously laid down on the inside of dolphin teeth. Each pair of rings, consisting of one light and one dark layer, corresponds to one year. The first layer forms before birth. This tooth is from a seven-year-old dolphin.

SOME POINTERS FOR PHOTOGRAPHING DOLPHINS

DOLPHINS are among the toughest animals to photograph well, but if you follow a few simple tips, you can spectacularly improve your chances. Almost everyone these days uses autofocus digital cameras, which have made it much easier to get good pictures.

- Digital 'point and shoot' cameras generally have a noticeable delay from when you press the shutter button to when the picture is actually taken. You can get great shots with a point and shoot, but it is certainly harder. You need to *anticipate* the action more.

- This delay is much shorter in Single Lens Reflex (SLR) cameras. If you can set the shutter speed on your camera, set it to 1/1000th of a second or faster, or use the 'sports programme' setting. Everything will be moving: the dolphins and the boat you are in, too. A high shutter speed will help freeze that movement.

- On a relatively bright day, set your camera's sensitivity to around 400 ISO. On a dull day you might need to go higher. This will make it easier to freeze the movement, gain more depth of field, and get good results from inexpensive lenses.

- Even if your camera has autofocus, it still needs your help. As you follow the dolphins in the viewfinder, press the shutter button down half way so that the camera is actively focusing on them, then when the moment comes, press the button fully. If you wait for the ideal moment without focusing and then press the button, the camera will focus first, then take the picture. Often, the dolphin will have gone by then and you will have photographed a splash. Not very satisfying.

- For most dolphins, an 80–200 mm zoom lens is an excellent choice for close-up pictures. While it does help, you don't need really fancy gear. The most important thing is to be out there, and ready.

GETTING TO KNOW THE DOLPHINS

WITHOUT DOUBT, the most powerful tool for studying dolphins is a good camera. In 1/1000th of a second a photographer can permanently record any marks and scars that make an individual dolphin distinctive. If we also note the time, date and location, we have the raw material to learn some very interesting things. By analysing resightings we can tell where dolphins go, who they hang around with and how often they give birth. With a little maths, we can use these resightings to calculate how many survive from year to year. All this, without touching the dolphins. And it is fun!

Several companies take people out dolphin-watching in Akaroa Harbour, Banks Peninsula, on the east coast of the South Island.

THE SOAP OPERA – WHAT PHOTO-ID CAN TELL US ABOUT DIFFERENT INDIVIDUALS

Several hundred individual NZ dolphins from the Banks Peninsula area have been identified photographically. The following 'biographies' of our best-known dolphins will give you an idea of what can be found out by long-term study.

Biggus Nickus is one of our best-known dolphins. We first photographed him in November 1984, in the first two weeks of starting our research on NZ dolphins, and saw him almost every year until 2001. Soon after that, he either died of old age or got caught in a fishing net. In 1984 he was already 4–5 years old, so he lived 20–25 years. His home range was a 29 km-long stretch of coastline on the south side of Banks Peninsula. He spent about half of his time between Birdlings Flat and Peraki Bay, a stretch of about 7 km of coastline. It is amazing for a dolphin to have such a small home range. Occasionally we saw him in small groups with one or two other males, but more often he was part of a larger group with other adults, sometimes including females and calves.

Biggus Nickus' official catalogue number was FSV.3025. His number starts with 'FSV' because he had several (SV) fin nicks (F). The numbers work like the book numbers in a library. Dolphins with similar markings are put close together in the catalogue (like books by the same author). The numbers are allocated in such a way as to leave enough space to put a new individual in between the two individuals it most resembles.

Originally Biggus Nickus had one large nick in his dorsal fin, which earned him his name (slightly modified from a character in Monty Python's film *Life of Brian*). In 1993 he gained a second notch in his dorsal fin, but it didn't take us long to recognise him. NZ dolphins seem to accumulate nicks slowly, and this sort of thing happens very rarely. In addition to the nicks in his dorsal fin, Biggus Nickus had several large dark blotches on his skin. These 'tattoo lesions' occur on many dolphin species worldwide, and appear to be caused by a pox virus. His spectacular fin nicks made it possible for us to follow changes in the tattoo marks to find out how reliable they are for long-term identification. Unlike leopards, dolphins slowly change their spots: tattoos change in size and shape gradually over the years. Recognising a tattooed dolphin from one year to the next is easy, but might not be possible if the sightings were five years apart. But even if his dorsal fin had been damaged beyond recognition, the skin blotches would have been sufficiently distinctive and long lasting for us still to recognise Biggus Nickus. Individuals with fin nicks as well as body markings are great for estimating the speed at which these features accumulate and change over time.

Punk (also known as FSV.3520) is one of the mature females in the photo-ID catalogue. She was first seen on 29 March 2000, and in the next eight years had one calf every two years. This makes her our star breeding female. Often female NZ dolphins take a three or four-year rest between calves. Punk is at least 20 years old now, and is nearing old age. In 2000, she was accompanied by a one-year-old calf. She must have been at least 7–9 years old at that time. This is the age at which female NZ dolphins give birth to their first calf. This calf stayed with her until at least November 2002. On 8 March 2004, she was seen with a new calf. This calf was still with her on 23 May 2005, but not 3 months later in August 2005.

Mothers suckle their young for up to one and a half years. During the first six months, the calf feeds only on milk. After that, the calf starts taking small fish and squid but still takes milk as and when the mother allows. For the first few months, mother and calf are rarely seen apart and the calf almost looks like it is attached by a rubber band. The calf becomes progressively more independent. By 18 months, it can feed itself entirely. Mature females are often accompanied by a one or two-year-old.

Rooster (FSVW.265) is another breeding female we saw with four different calves. We called her Rooster before we knew she was a female, because her fin nicks looked like a rooster's wattle. She is no longer alive, but was already mature when we first saw her in 1986. Rooster had a newborn calf in January 1988, which was still with her in January 1989. Her next calf was born in January 1992, and was still with her in January 1993. Two more calves were born, in December 1993 and January 1995. In February 1996 she was seen with that calf, then a yearling, and that was the last time we saw her. If Rooster died of natural causes, that suggests NZ dolphins continue to breed well into old age. That is likely, in any case, for an animal with a relatively short lifespan (25 years or so). Some longer-lived whales and dolphins are known to have a post-reproductive period (like humans). For example, pilot whales live to about 60 years old, but stop breeding around 40.

Photograph: Will Rayment.

Huffer

Photographs: Will Rayment.

Sharkbait

Huffer was given this name because he has three dark circles on the front of his body that look like the three dots in the Huffer logo. His most distinctive feature is a W-shaped nick out of the dorsal fin – which is why his catalogue number is FSVW.300. All dolphins with FSV in their number have several fin nicks. The FSVW dolphins have a nick that looks like a W. Huffer's fin nick looks like it was caused by a bite, but not necessarily a bite from another dolphin. Huffer has been seen more than 20 times since 2003. His home range is a 21 km stretch of coastline on the north side of Banks Peninsula and he is most often seen between Pigeon Bay and Port Levy.

Huffer has been seen following trawlers around. On most of our surveys on the north side of Banks Peninsula, we see one or two small trawlers between Godley Head and Pigeon Bay. These trawlers catch a mix of flatfish, red cod, gurnard and other species. Often a group of dolphins and seabirds (including shags and seagulls) follows the trawler around. Dolphin groups following trawlers tend to be much larger, with around 20–25 rather than the usual 2–8 individuals. Aside from feeding, there are commonly a lot of social interactions, including sexual behaviour. Often we can see the trawl net on the echosounder of our research boat, and occasionally we can see the dolphins diving towards the net. The dolphins feed on fish that have escaped the net, including fish being stirred up by the net that have managed to escape its mouth or are small enough to pass through the mesh. Feeding round trawl nets is not without risk, and some dolphins get caught and drown.

It's obvious how Sharkbait (FSV.7790, opposite) got his name. We have several shark attack survivors in the ID catalogue, as well as some gillnet entanglement survivors. These are of course the lucky ones. Shark bites are often on the dorsal fin and the area immediately behind the fin. Apparently the dolphins twist away during a shark attack so that their more solid dorsal side gets bitten, rather than their much more vulnerable belly. Of course, then the dolphin has to make a run for it and hope it can either outrun or outwit the shark. As you can see from the photos, even very serious injuries can heal reasonably quickly. When Sharkbait was first seen on 19 January 2003, his wounds were still fresh, looking pink and white. By December 2003 they were already well healed (bottom left).

We know Sharkbait is a male because we have seen him on underwater video. Sometimes we get lucky and a dolphin with distinctive markings swims upside down close to the boat, but many of the individuals of known sex have been identified in Trudi Webster's work with the 'polecam', a small video camera in an underwater housing. It is attached to a window-washing pole and is usually used at the bow of the boat while the boat is very slowly moving forwards (see photo p. 27). With a bit of luck, the dolphins come to bowride. If we can get a good look at the belly, and on the same bit of video can see the identifying markings (such as fin nicks or skin coloration), then another individual of known gender can go into the catalogue. The next few pages give just a few examples from our ID catalogue.

BBT.010 Known as 'Zorro' by the researchers and 'the Caped Crusader' by the dolphin-watching guides, this NZ dolphin is often seen in Akaroa Harbour. On 27 January 2008, Trudi Webster found out he is male, by using a small video camera on a pole to take a close look at him underwater.

BBW.0390 This dolphin, with a young calf at her side, is one of 82 individuals in our catalogue with unusual white body markings. Some have only one or two small white marks, but this mature female and a few others look like someone has thrown a bucket of white paint at them. These marks change very slowly over time, but allow us to identify the individual for many years or even decades.

BS4.010 This fresh wound is almost certainly from a shark attack. It is possible that the three puncture wounds in front of the dorsal fin are from teeth in the shark's upper jaw, while the wound was caused by teeth in the lower jaw. If so, this suggests a large shark and a lucky escape. We have seen similar puncture wounds on other NZ dolphins that have more typical-looking shark bites (e.g. Sharkbait on p. 58).

FL67.2480 This female was first seen in 2003 and is most often seen in Akaroa Harbour, Flea Bay, Island Bay and along the south side of Banks Peninsula.

FSV.3065 It is not clear what caused the damage to this dolphin's fin, and the scar behind the fin. Both were fresh in January 2007 and well healed in January 2008. We know this individual as 'Pete B'.

FSV.3055 This male dolphin, known as 'Fingers' by the dolphin-watching guides, appears to be another shark attack survivor. The tattered dorsal fin, and other scarring behind the fin, look like typical shark bites.

Fingers is often seen in Akaroa Harbour, Flea Bay, Whakamoa Reef and occasionally also on the east side of Banks Peninsula near Le Bons Bay.

This large scar was caused by a piece of nylon line or gillnet that this dolphin became caught in, and which became embedded in the flesh before breaking and pulling out. There are six other individuals in the Banks Peninsula photo-ID catalogue with these kinds of 'encircling' scars, and these have also been seen in other dolphin species.

The sharp cuts in this dolphin's fin are most likely caused by a gillnet. Several of the dolphins in the catalogue have sharp cuts like this in the dorsal fin, often at regular intervals, indicating the spacing of the meshes of the net.

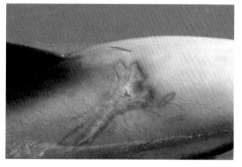

Individuals with more than one nick are especially useful for photo-ID. They are more likely to remain recognisable, even if the dorsal fin is modified by further damage.

We are not sure what caused the deep scar on this dolphin. It is possible it was caused by the dolphin colliding with trawl gear – NZ dolphins regularly feed around trawl nets – but we can't be sure. There are two individuals in the catalogue with a similar scar on the same part of the body.

Sharp cuts like this in the dorsal fin are unlikely to have a natural cause. Most likely the fin damage was caused by nylon line, either as fishing line or part of a monofilament gillnet.

This dolphin has a beautifully distinctive dorsal fin, with several nicks, and was only one year old when first photographed, so has already been in the wars. The small brown dots on its side are not useful for identification. These are cyamids or 'whale lice'.

The fin nick on this dolphin will be distinctive for years to come. The toothrakes on the left side of the dolphin, below and in front of the dorsal fin, will heal in just a few weeks and are not useful for identification.

The 'tattoo' lesions on the body of this dolphin are thought to be caused by a pox virus. Similar marks are seen on many other dolphin species, and they appear to do no harm. Tattoo marks change slowly over time, but last many years and can be useful for photo-ID.

Huffer completing a horizontal jump.

TO TAG OR NOT TO TAG?

From time to time, people ask us if we tag the dolphins. It's not easy to tag dolphins. They don't have necks, so attaching a collar won't work. The outer layer of their skin constantly sloughs off (it's how they avoid fouling animals like barnacles) so you cannot glue a tag to their skin, as you can with a seal or sea lion. Instead, tags are bolted onto the dorsal fin, and for that you have to catch the dolphin first. That's not easy, and has substantial risks for the dolphin.

We don't use tagging, for three reasons. The first reason is ethical: we don't think it is acceptable to harm a study animal unless doing so is of direct benefit to that individual, or its species. Just as in medical research, there has to be a compelling argument that the outcome is for the 'greater good'. The second reason is scientific: tagging often changes the behaviour of the animal that is tagged, so the researcher is left unsure about whether its behaviour is normal or corrupted by its response to the tag, or the tagging. The third objection is simply practical. There are already several hundred, individually recognisable NZ dolphins around Banks Peninsula. For a decent photographer, each of those is already tagged.

CONSERVATION PROBLEMS AND SOLUTIONS

PROBLEM – GILLNETS

Unfortunately, several features of NZ dolphins make them very vulnerable to human impacts. The total population is small, and fragmented into many smaller, local populations. Their coastal distribution puts them precisely in the zone where human activities are most intensive. Also, dolphins in general, and NZ dolphins especially, have very low reproductive rates.

Entanglement of marine mammals in gillnets is a worldwide problem. Thirty-nine of the world's 42 species of dolphins and porpoises are known to be killed in gillnets. The remaining three are either large (such as the killer whale), very rare (such as the spectacled porpoise) or have subantarctic distributions (such as the hourglass dolphin) well away from gillnetting fleets. Each year, several hundred thousand dolphins and porpoises are killed in gillnets worldwide. In comparison, all other impacts, including pollution, hunting, habitat loss and climate change, pale almost into insignificance. Open-ocean driftnets, each one up to 60 km long, have attracted a lot of attention, but a less conspicuous form of gillnetting – in which the nets are anchored on the bottom – is more prevalent around the world and has a much greater impact. In part, this is because the dolphins they entangle are coastal species, like the NZ dolphin, which have smaller distributions and smaller populations than their oceanic relatives.

In 1984, when we started our research, we thought we might find a small number of dolphins to dissect so we could learn a little about their biology. We put the word around fishers and asked them to pass on any dolphins they found dead in their nets. Some were very helpful, and soon we were dissecting far more dolphins than we ever expected. At this point we realised that the focus of our research needed to shift, so that we could assess what impact these catches were having. In addition to ageing dolphins and studying their reproduction, we began to interview fishers to find out how many were being caught. We also kept an ear to the ground, and recovered dead dolphins from beaches whenever we could.

Simply adding up the number of dolphin catches the fishers told us about caused a great deal of concern. Between 1984 and 1988, 230 NZ dolphins were reported killed in gillnets between Motunau, 60 km north of Banks Peninsula, and Timaru, some 150 km to the south. At the time, the interview data were heavily criticised, but there have been two further studies, one using independent observers on fishing boats, and one using automatically activated video cameras in place of observers.

NZ dolphin caught in an amateur gillnet in 2001 near Granity, Buller Bay, near the northern end of the west coast of the South Island.

WHAT IS A GILLNET?

A GILLNET is a wall of netting, usually with small weights along the bottom and floats along the top so that the net forms a vertical 'wall' in the water. It can either be set on the bottom and anchored at each end (a 'setnet' or 'bottom-set gillnet') or left drifting, usually near the surface (a 'driftnet'). The name 'gillnet' derives from its design – fish swimming through the net are caught by the gills ('gilling') or entangled in several meshes.

Gillnetting is cheap. Fuel costs are low because the nets are not towed, and gillnets catch a wide range of fish species. They are selective at the lower end of the size range (fish smaller than the mesh size are seldom caught), but not at the upper end (anything larger than the mesh size can be caught – right up to whales). Mesh size and net length vary widely, depending on the target species.

Apart from their much greater length, and being set to drift, open-ocean driftnets are not fundamentally different from the bottom-set gillnets used in New Zealand. By removing the anchors, and decreasing the weight of the lead-line at the bottom of the net, any gillnet can be made into a driftnet. Driftnets up to one kilometre long are legal in New Zealand waters.

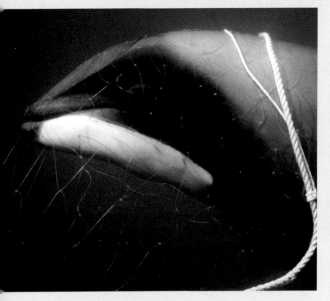 

A NZ dolphin drowned in a net (left), and a new 'recreational' gillnet being prepared.

Photograph: Roger Grace

While gillnets have been around for more than 2000 years, from the 1960s two technological changes caused a spectacular expansion in their use worldwide. First, nylon monofilament mesh replaced cotton. Because nylon does not rot, the new nets have a much longer life – a fact that causes problems when nets are lost. Second, net hauling, previously done manually, became mechanised, with hydraulic motors powering net drums or line haulers. Fishers could set several kilometres of net from small (<15 m) boats. These two changes, along with a policy of unlimited access (anyone could buy a license and go fishing commercially) and high fish prices, caused a rapid expansion of inshore gillnetting in New Zealand, peaking in the mid to late 1970s. No one knows how many dolphins died in that gillnet-rush. Since the mid 1980s, gillnetting in shallow water (less than 100 m deep – where the risk to dolphins is greatest) has declined, thanks to the introduction of the Quota Management System and the dolphin protection measures.

Unfortunately gillnets, whether set in shallow water on the bottom or left to drift, are devastatingly effective at catching dolphins. The clearest demonstration of this is shown by Peru's illegal dolphin 'fishery', which killed several thousand dolphins each year for human consumption. For catching dolphins, these fishers chose driftnets or bottom-set gillnets as their most effective methods.

A gillnet catching what it is intended to. These moki are a frequent target for amateur gillnetters.

Gillnets used by amateur (or 'recreational' fishers) can catch a surprisingly large number of NZ dolphins. These four dolphins were caught in 2005, in one amateur gillnet at Neil's Beach, Jackson Bay, towards the southern end of the west coast of the South Island.

Photograph: Department of Conservation.

The studies using video cameras and observers on fishing boats produced even higher estimates of catch rate than the interviews, and showed unequivocally that there was a serious entanglement problem.

Worldwide, many other biologists have had similar experiences. For example, when he encouraged fishers to bring dead porpoises back for dissection, Andy Read (now a professor at Duke University) was practically swamped. A consistent observation is that until someone actively solicits information, or an observer programme is put in place, bycatch is seldom reported. This is not surprising. There is no incentive to do so.

By the late 1980s, it was clear that the dolphins in the Banks Peninsula area were being caught at a rate that was unsustainable. This conclusion was based on several independent pieces of evidence. Our work on reproduction and population

biology showed that the likely maximum population growth rate was around 2 per cent per year. The survival rates of NZ dolphins were simply not high enough for the population to be able to grow. We also used the guidelines for sustainable levels of human impacts on marine mammals in the USA. The US guidelines were developed by a team of experts, and were based on detailed knowledge of the reproductive rates of dolphins and porpoises. The number of dolphins taken each year around Banks Peninsula far exceeded these guidelines.

Later research confirmed that NZ dolphins were in trouble. The National Institute for Water and Atmosphere estimated that during the years 2000–2006, 110–150 NZ dolphins were caught in gillnets each year. Most entanglements were in commercial fishing nets, but amateur gillnetters, typically setting nets for moki, butterfish or flounder, were also exacting a toll, especially before the protection at Banks Peninsula came into being in 1988. It was hard to convince them that they were part of the problem, because for each fisher the chance of catching a dolphin was very small. But there were many fishers. If, for example, amateur gillnet fishers each caught one dolphin every thirty years or so, many would not have caught a dolphin at all, and any one of them would likely feel that their impact was small. However, 300 amateur fishers might catch, on average, ten dolphins per year. The number of amateur gillnetters fishing around Banks Peninsula is unknown, but one morning in December 1987 we counted 66 gillnets set in just three bays in the upper reaches of Akaroa Harbour (Duvauchelle, Robinsons and Takamatua Bays).

SOLUTIONS

In 1988 Helen Clark, then Minister of Conservation, created the Banks Peninsula Marine Mammal Sanctuary. In a 1170 km^2 area stretching from Sumner Head just north of Banks Peninsula, to the Rakaia River, and out to 4 nautical miles (7.4 km) offshore, gillnetting on a commercial scale was banned. New rules were designed for amateur gillnetters, to further reduce dolphin entanglements. All other commercial and amateur fishing methods were unaffected. Line fishing, fish traps and most other fishing methods were allowed to continue. Likewise, it remains legal today to use a gillnet as a dragnet for catching flounder, or as a ring net (encircling gillnet) for catching mullet.

Our research has shown that the Banks Peninsula Marine Mammal Sanctuary was a major step in the right direction. Using more than 20 years of Photo-ID data, Andrew Gormley, then one of our PhD students, showed that the survival rates of the dolphins around Banks Peninsula has increased by more than 5 per cent. That doesn't sound like much, but it makes a big difference. Before the sanctuary was created, the dolphin population was declining rapidly. It is still declining today, but very slowly, so that's major progress. It shows that reducing the overlap between dolphins and gillnets works.

Another research project, examining offshore distribution of the dolphins, shows what needs to be done now to allow the population first to stabilise and then to recover from past impacts. Research by Will Rayment, another of our PhD students, showed that the dolphins around Banks Peninsula range out to 20 nautical miles offshore, yet the protection measures extend to only 4 nautical miles offshore. In summer, when the dolphins spend a lot of time close to shore, about 80 per cent of the population is within 4 nautical miles from shore. But in winter this drops to only about 40 per cent. Extending the offshore boundaries of the protected area to match the dolphins' distribution would solve the problem.

The next step in protecting NZ dolphins was taken in 2003. Pete Hodgson, then Minister of Fisheries, created a protected area off the North Island west coast. The fishing industry took him to court and, after much debate, the harbours (except for the entrance of the Manukau harbour) and the southern part of the dolphins' distribution were left out of the protection measures. It is now clear that without fixing those two loopholes, the North

Island population is unlikely to survive. Recent dolphin sightings and deaths in gillnets off the Taranaki coastline show that the protected area boundaries are not yet in the right place.

The third step – taken in 2008 by Jim Anderton, then Minister of Fisheries – was by far the biggest. As a result, we now have a much more comprehensive package of measures, with at least some protection in most areas where NZ dolphins are found. The decision was preceded by lengthy public consultation and discussion with the fishing industry. And, yet again, it was followed by the Minister being taken to court by the fishing industry. Several compromises were made. Gillnetting still continues in several 'exemption' areas, including the North Island harbours, Tasman Bay, Golden Bay and parts of the Kaikoura and Marlborough coastlines. Discussions continue on closing these 'loopholes' in the protection measures.

The species as a whole is listed as **Endangered** by national (Department of Conservation) and international (International Union for Conservation of Nature) agencies. The North Island population, also known as Maui's dolphin, is listed separately as **Critically Endangered**. The only worse category is **Extinct**. By definition, the North Island population is at an extremely high risk of extinction. The most recent population estimate is about 55 Maui's dolphins aged one year and older. To put that into perspective, consider that about half of those 55 individuals will be female. So, about 27 females. Studies of other NZ dolphin populations indicate that about half of those will be mature, breeding females. That's about 14.

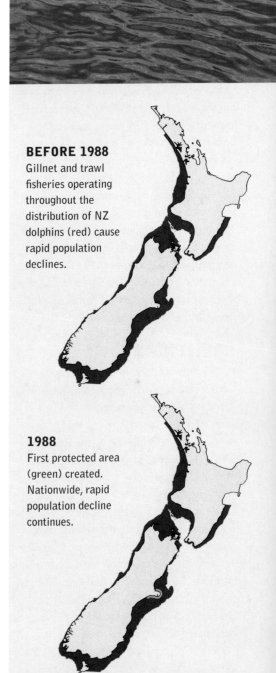

BEFORE 1988
Gillnet and trawl fisheries operating throughout the distribution of NZ dolphins (red) cause rapid population declines.

1988
First protected area (green) created. Nationwide, rapid population decline continues.

WHAT HAS BEEN DONE SO FAR TO PROTECT NZ DOLPHINS?

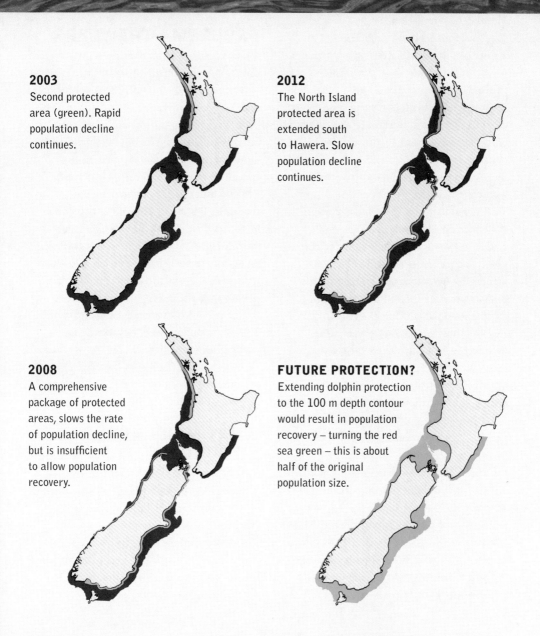

2003
Second protected area (green). Rapid population decline continues.

2012
The North Island protected area is extended south to Hawera. Slow population decline continues.

2008
A comprehensive package of protected areas, slows the rate of population decline, but is insufficient to allow population recovery.

FUTURE PROTECTION?
Extending dolphin protection to the 100 m depth contour would result in population recovery – turning the red sea green – this is about half of the original population size.

It is easy to see that the loss of just one female Maui's dolphin, perhaps in a gillnet set in one of the unprotected harbour areas, or around Taranaki, would be a very serious blow to the population.

A dolphin death off Cape Egmont in 2012 led to the fourth step taken to better protect NZ dolphins. The Minister for Primary Industries, David Carter, extended the protected area off the North Island west coast further south, to Hawera – and banned gillnets in this area to 2 nautical miles offshore. Independent observers are required on any vessels using gillnets between 2 and 7 nautical miles offshore.

The number of dolphins that continue to be seen outside protected areas and caught in fishing nets shows that the current protection measures are still not effective. Under the current protection measures, populations are expected to continue to decline – a slower decline than before 2008, certainly, but population decline rather than recovery. Risk analyses carried out by university and government scientists, as well as researchers working for the fishing industry, all show that NZ dolphin populations have declined rapidly since 1970 and that effective protection would result in population recovery.

The protection measures put in place so far have slowed the population decline, but are not yet sufficient to allow NZ dolphin populations to recover from the depletion that has occurred in the last 50 years. Extending protection from bycatch in both gillnets and trawling to the 100 m depth contour would result in population recovery to about half of the original population size (15,000) within 50 years. Conservation groups have called this 'turning the red sea green' (see maps on pp. 70–71).

PROBLEM – TRAWLERS

Most people understand the need to protect dolphins from gillnets. This problem has been well documented both in NZ and worldwide, and the benefits of reducing the overlap between dolphins and gillnets have been clearly demonstrated for NZ dolphins. There is greater debate about managing inshore trawling. Trawlers catch dolphins in New Zealand waters as they do in other parts of the world. It is clear from voluntary reports by fishers that NZ dolphins are also caught in trawl fisheries. The level of observer coverage on inshore trawlers has been too low to make it possible to estimate the total number of NZ dolphins caught, but captures have been noted by independent observers carried on board. The catch rate appears to be much lower for trawlers than for gillnetters, but this is offset by a much larger number of trawling vessels. A precautionary decision would be to avoid both trawling and gillnets in dolphin habitat.

WHAT MORE NEEDS TO BE DONE?

The Scientific Committee of the International Whaling Commission has addressed bycatch of NZ dolphins several times since 1984. In 2012, the Scientific Committee – a group of 164 international experts on whales and dolphins – discussed the threat of extinction for the North Island (Maui's dolphin) population and recommended:

NZ dolphins are often seen following trawlers, in this case off Godley Head on the north side of Banks Peninsula. The Christchurch suburbs of Scarborough and Redcliffs are visible behind the fishing boat. The dolphins may follow the fishing boat for hours, staying just behind where the net is – and diving down to feed on what the net stirred up but did not catch.

Left: This dolphin has approached the boat while the net is being hauled aboard. The cod end of the net is still in the water.

- An immediate extension of the North Island protected area south to Hawera.
- An immediate extension offshore to the 100 m depth contour.
- Inclusion of North Island harbours in the protected area.
- Protection from both gillnet and trawl fisheries.
- Protection of the northern coast of the South Island, to provide a conservation 'corridor' between North and South Island.

The Minister for Primary Industries followed the Scientific Committee's first recommendation, extending the protected area south to Hawera and banning gillnets to 2 nautical miles offshore. Unfortunately, the Scientific Committee's four other recommendations were ignored. In addition to receiving this clear advice from scientific experts, the Minister had a clear mandate from the New Zealand public. Consultation before the Minister made his decision resulted in 24,448 public submissions asking that all five of the above protection measures be implemented. By comparison, 31 of the submissions wanted no additional dolphin protection and five submissions supported the Minister's decision. The risk of extinction for the North Island population could be reduced substantially by following all of the recommendations from the IWC.

Protection of the North Island Maui's dolphin population is the most urgent priority for putting the species as a whole on the road to recovery. Losing this population would mean losing a very large part of the overall distribution of NZ dolphins, as they are already absent, or very rare, in large parts of their former North Island range. For example, today NZ dolphins are only very occasionally seen in Wellington Harbour and on the Wairarapa and Kapiti coastlines.

The continuing fragmentation of the distribution of NZ dolphins is a risk factor in itself (see section on Distribution p. 12). So what needs to be done to avoid further fragmentation? It would make sense to ban amateur gillnetting throughout New Zealand. Recreational fishers are not allowed to use gillnets in most other 'developed' countries. Our experience has been that amateur gillnetters often set their nets inappropriately (for example with plastic milk bottles as floats) so they are prone to loss in bad weather. Further, gillnets are inherently unselective (for example, flounder nets routinely catch stingrays), and pose serious risks to diving birds (shags, penguins and shearwaters) as well as to dolphins. Most recreational boats are too small to send along a fisheries observer. This makes it difficult and very expensive to collect accurate information on how many dolphins are caught by amateur fishers.

Conservation groups have been advocating a 'gillnet-free New Zealand'. In 2012, a coalition of 20 conservation groups wrote to the New Zealand government calling for gillnets and trawling to be banned in all areas where NZ dolphins are found. The coalition included New Zealand and international conservation groups: American Cetacean Society, Animal Welfare Institute, Blue Voice, Cetacean Society International, Earth Island Institute, Earthrace Conservation Organization, Greenpeace, Humane Society International, NABU International, Foundation for Nature, Nantucket Marine Mammal Conservation Program, Natural Resources Defense Council, Origami Whales Project, Project Jonah, Royal Forest and Bird Protection Society of New Zealand, Save the Whales Again!, Sea Shepherd Conservation Society, The Whaleman Foundation, Whale and Dolphin Conservation Society, Whales Need US Coalition, World Society for the Protection of Animals, and World Wide Fund for Nature.

Biologically, it is clear that banning gillnetting and trawling would benefit not only NZ dolphins, but also other species like common dolphins, bottlenose dolphins, dusky dolphins, penguins, shags and other seabird species, as well as sharks and fish. The conservation coalition is asking the New Zealand government to 'turn the red sea green' (see maps on pp. 70–71).

The good news is that solving this

Some of the loopholes in the current protection measures are based on the assumption that NZ dolphins do not use close inshore habitats where fishers set nets for butterfish, in and around kelp beds. As can be seen above, this argument doesn't make sense.

conservation problem is relatively simple. The most serious threat has been identified and could easily be removed. More than a decade of discussion involving the fishing industry, the Ministry for Primary Industries, Department of Conservation and independent experts has identified deaths in fishing gear as the number one threat. This was confirmed by an Expert Panel in 2012. The panel was appointed by the Ministry for Primary Industries and Department of Conservation, and consisted of scientists from Otago University, Auckland University, the National Institute for Water and Atmosphere, Te Papa Tongarewa (New Zealand's national museum), the Seafood Industry Council and the US National Marine Fisheries Service. The panel confirmed that bycatch in gillnet and trawl fisheries is still the most serious risk to NZ dolphins.

OTHER THREATS

While bycatch in fishing is clearly the most important threat to NZ dolphins, there are other impacts. Human-made chemicals like PCBs, DDTs and dioxins have been found in the tissues of NZ dolphins at higher levels than in other wildlife. These chemicals are known to affect reproduction in marine mammals, in some cases causing reduced reproductive success. Concentrations known to cause serious health impacts to marine mammals elsewhere, for example in the USA, Canada, Japan and the North Sea, are much higher than those in New Zealand. While we cannot be certain that local levels of toxins are causing harm, it is fair to assume they are not helping.

Other human activities, such as sand mining, coastal development, increasing vessel traffic and proposals for developing tidal turbines in dolphin habitat, are potential threats. We do not have enough information to determine how serious these impacts might become in the future but, again, it is unlikely they will help.

Dolphin tourism can cause harassment. We are much less concerned about tour boats than about unthinking folks out in their own boats. Tourism pressure on NZ dolphins in Akaroa Harbour is high, much higher than on dusky dolphins at Kaikoura, for example. Wildlife tourism, however, by educating its clients about the dolphins and their habitat, has potential positive effects. There is no doubt that dolphin-watching tourism in Akaroa has played a large part in raising awareness about NZ dolphins, and their conservation problems. Making sure that tourism gives something back to the animals that sustain the business requires a strong educational programme.

All wildlife populations suffer predation, parasites and disease. Shark predation certainly occurs. Remains of NZ dolphins have been found in blue sharks and seven-gilled sharks, and some of the scars we see on live dolphins are large enough to implicate great

white sharks. Killer whales are known to take other dolphin species in our waters; while they have not been seen preying on NZ dolphins, they probably would, given the chance.

In autopsies, we have seen parasites commonly, but not at levels likely to endanger health. Roundworms (especially *Anisakis* sp) and flatworms (especially *Braunina condiformis*) are often seen in the stomach, usually in low numbers. Lungworms are sometimes present. Between the blubber and muscle, especially around the belly and genital area, we often find strange white cysts that are the larval stage of the flatworm *Phyllobothrium delphini*. This parasite *relies* on the fact that sharks attack dolphins, because the adult parasite can develop and reproduce only in the digestive system of sharks.

Most of the 120 or so NZ dolphins we have dissected were killed in fishing gear, and were otherwise healthy. Dolphins, however, like us or any other animal, suffer many diseases. Most are trivial, such as the pox virus that causes the tattoo lesions that help us identify individuals. These seem to have no health consequences – a bit like warts in humans. Recently, two more serious diseases have been found. *Brucella* bacteria have been found in almost every dolphin species so far screened (as well as whales and seals) – including NZ dolphins. *Brucella* can cause abortion in pregnant females. It appears to be a naturally occurring pathogen that marine mammals have evolved with over many thousands of years. Toxoplasmosis is another disease found in NZ dolphins, by veterinarians at Massey University. This is caused by a single-celled parasite and has recently been identified in 9 of 31 NZ dolphins that were tested for the antibodies – which indicate exposure. Depending on which strain of Toxoplasma you come into contact with, the parasite can be of minor inconvenience in humans – producing flu-like symptoms for a few days – but can also cause abortion. If the immune system is compromised, some strains of Toxoplasma can cause life-threatening disease. The strain present in NZ dolphins has not yet been identified. Cats are the parasite's usual primary host, and contact with cat faeces is the usual path of infection in humans. Again, this disease is very common in humans as well as whales and dolphins. Because cats were introduced to New Zealand by Europeans, Toxoplasmosis may be relatively new to NZ dolphins.

Disease, parasites and predation are part of the environment that dolphins evolved in. Indeed, the very reason why dolphins have some potential for population growth is that these natural threats do not cause extinction. It is also important to note that these impacts are unmanageable. Realistically, there is nothing we can do about them. In our view, the existence of natural impacts makes it all the more important to reduce the impacts we *can* manage.

The evidence is very clear that NZ dolphins were much more common 50 years ago than they are now, and that the largest single factor in their decline is mortality in fishing nets. We humans are the problem. We need to be the solution.

IN CONCLUSION

In thinking about impacts on dolphins, or on anything else, it is crucially important to keep a sense of perspective. We need to address the most serious impacts first, and not get diverted away from these. For NZ dolphins, a sensible management approach would be to keep fisheries bycatch *well below* sustainable levels, because there are other, additional, but less important, threats.

NZ dolphins are one of New Zealand's great natural assets. They are absolutely remarkable animals: as 'kiwi' as the kiwi. Rare, fascinating and attractive, they are threatened only by *our* impact. Our fishing causes the entanglements, and the dangerous pollutants they accumulate come only from us. The species is endangered and we need to take every reasonable step to reduce our impacts. They do not need captive breeding or any other intensive management – we simply need to stop killing dolphins in fishing nets and go a bit easier on their environment.

The take-home message is that dolphin deaths in fishing gear are avoidable. Dolphin-safe fishing methods exist, and are better for fish stocks too. Making the transition to more selective, sustainable fishing methods would not only save the NZ dolphin, but also benefit the fishing industry itself. In addition to avoiding the bad press associated with killing dolphins, seals and seabirds, shifting to more selective methods would promote healthier fish stocks. Surely we can solve this problem – it does not seem much to ask.

WHAT YOU CAN DO TO HELP

HOW TO SUPPORT CONSERVATION EFFORTS

- Do not use gillnets – use fishing lines, fish traps, small dragnets, hand gathering or spearfishing instead.
- When buying fish, ask how it was caught. Do not buy fish that was caught in a gillnet.
- Become involved. Ask several conservation groups what they are doing to help save NZ dolphins, and consider supporting the group that gives the best answer.
- Talk to friends, family and other interested people.
- Use email, the internet, Facebook and other social media to get the word out as widely as possible.
- Ask the Minister of Conservation and the Minister for Primary Production what they are doing to help save NZ dolphins. Don't accept a 'PR' answer. Insist on knowing exactly what they are doing, and urge them to do (much) more.
- Support research and conservation by making a donation to the NZ Whale and Dolphin Trust.

DOLPHIN ETIQUETTE

A key reason why dolphins are so popular is that they are friendly. They are attracted to boats, and are very curious. You can encourage them to spend more time with you if you 'behave yourself'.

Some suggestions for good etiquette are on the following two pages. It is simply common sense and it all comes down to showing some respect for these marvellous animals. We cannot speak their language, so all they have to go by is our actions.

Please look where you are going. This boat driver isn't.

IF YOU ARE IN A BOAT

- Approach slowly from the side or rear of the group. Try not to split the group by driving through the middle.
- Avoid sudden changes in speed or direction. Sudden turns or acceleration may put dolphins at risk from your propeller, or simply frighten them. Often, the best speed is the slowest your engine will go.
- Never use reverse among or towards dolphins.
- Do not repeatedly approach dolphins that don't seem to be interested in your boat.
- Take special care with groups containing mothers and calves. These groups are normally less interested in boats. Unless they approach you, consider leaving them alone.
- Try turning off your engine, and waiting. When we are trying to photograph dolphins that are busy and not interested in the boat, we often use the 'Milo method'. This highly successful technique, perfected over several decades of research, consists of stopping the boat, having a cup of Milo, and waiting for them to come to us. It also works with coffee and soup.
- When you leave the group, start slowly and accelerate very gradually.
- Stick to the rules. To minimise harassment, there are some legal restrictions on what you can do around dolphins. For more information, contact your local Department of Conservation office.
- It should go without saying, but you should avoid dropping litter in the water. Marine mammals are occasionally found entangled in discarded plastic or with plastic in their stomachs.

IF YOU WANT TO SWIM WITH DOLPHINS

SWIMMING WITH DOLPHINS can be a fabulous experience, but NZ dolphins often find swimmers a bit threatening, and sometimes avoid coming very close. They are, after all, smaller than you are, and in the wild it makes sense to be wary of anything big. To have a successful swim, you need to avoid any behaviours that might seem threatening.

You can swim with NZ dolphins from your own boat, or take a commercial dolphin swimming trip in Akaroa Harbour.

- Enter the water gently, and try to swim smoothly. In our experience splashing does not help.
- Do not try to touch the dolphins. If you do, generally they will stay further away, well out of reach. If you are very lucky, they will touch you. Leave it to them.
- NZ dolphins often seem more relaxed if your behaviour is predictable. For example, they are often highly curious of a swimmer who is being towed slowly on a rope. Part of this may be because a towed swimmer cannot chase them, and therefore seems less threatening.

Opposite page: The photograph on the far left shows another example of a wrong approach: In any boat, watching where you are going is crucial! If you want a good look, slow down to an idle or stop, and let the dolphins come to you, as shown in the other two photographs.

WHAT HAPPENS ON A TYPICAL DAY OF NZ DOLPHIN RESEARCH?

THE ALARM CLOCK goes off at dawn. Two of them, actually. The bellbirds start their loud dawn chorus outside. But if that's not enough to wake us up, the rather less melodious alarm clock will make sure of it. In the middle of summer, dawn is at about 5.30 am. In summer, we joke about 'working 5 to 9' (the reverse of the Dolly Parton song).

You need good light for dolphin surveys, and for photography, so there's little point in pre-dawn starts. But the weather is almost always much calmer first thing in the morning, so it's well worth getting up early. After checking the weather forecast, including swell, winds predicted for the day and actual wind speed at Le Bons Bay (automatically recorded every three hours), we decide whether to go out in the boat, and where to go. If we can hear wind outside or rain on the roof, we just turn the alarm clock off and go back to sleep.

If it's a good day for fieldwork, we stumble through the routine of breakfast, lunch making, and so on, and launch the boat. Once we get going, we turn on the VHF radio, the Global Positioning System (GPS) navigator and a tiny Hewlett-Packard computer. The GPS shows us precisely where we are throughout the day, on a chart of the area, and sends its data to the computer. The computer, housed in a splashproof case with a silicone rubber membrane over the keyboard, records our track (and depth and sea temperature), so that we have a precise record of where we have been and for how long. When we encounter dolphins, a keypress grabs the date, time and position fix from the GPS, then the computer prompts us for data on group size, number of calves and weather conditions, and allows us to make whatever notes are needed.

Today we are doing a photo-ID survey of the area from Akaroa Harbour to Birdlings Flat, a round trip distance of about 40 nautical miles (74 km). We keep a very sharp lookout for dolphins and photograph any with distinctive markings. This trip is one we've done many times, and is one of our favourites. The south side of Banks Peninsula is spectacularly scenic, sheltered from the prevailing northeasterlies and, most important, is prime NZ dolphin country.

On another day we might survey the north or east side of the peninsula, or go a little further afield. The main goal is to photograph as many distinctive dolphins as possible. As outlined in Chapter 8, good ID photographs can provide information on reproduction, survival, movement and associations.

For our photo-ID surveys we travel roughly 400 m offshore along the open coast, and we go into each bay. Our 15-knot survey speed is a good compromise between being fast enough to cover long distances reasonably quickly, and slow enough to have

The authors at work off the coast of Banks Peninsula.

a good chance of seeing most of the dolphins (you will always miss some). Today, we start the survey at Birdlings Flat. Having travelled there 'off effort' we will now be 'on effort' searching for dolphins for the rest of the day, from Birdlings Flat to Akaroa.

It's not long before we see the first group of dolphins, off Oashore Bay. We approach and the dolphins head straight for us. They seem to enjoy riding underneath our bow, especially at slow speeds between 1 and 5 knots. If any are recognisable, perhaps with a nick or scar, Steve snaps off pictures in quick succession as they surface near the boat. The pictures have to be pin-sharp to be useful, and as exactly side-on as possible. The dolphins typically surface for about a second, so the photographer needs to be on

the ball to get the pictures needed. A good boat driver is important, too – the idea is to anticipate where that particular dolphin will surface next and position the boat for a good shot. We change speed as little as possible. The camera is really our primary research tool – with it we gather most of our data. Once we have the pictures we need, we enter notes into the computer and leave the group. Often the dolphins follow, surfing in our wake or bowriding. Sometimes we need to speed up a little to leave them behind. If they catch up when we're stopped with the next group, things can get quite confusing.

We continue heading along the south side of the peninsula, going into the bays. Almost always we find dolphins in the mile or so between at Oashore Bay and Hikuraki

Bay, as well as other groups scattered along the coast. Surfers riding the ocean swells near Hikuraki Bay often surf with dolphins, and probably wonder just what we are doing idling back and forth among the dolphins outside the shore break. Usually the groups of dolphins are small, numbering fewer than a dozen individuals, but we've seen some of our largest groups here, with more than 50 scattered over an area a few hundred metres across. It's more difficult working with the larger groups, as they are difficult to count and it's hard to keep track of any particular dolphin we need to photograph.

Beautiful Te Oka Bay, deeply indented with a pebbly beach at its end, often has one or two groups of dolphins. This general area used to be Biggus Nickus' territory (see p. 56). 'Al Dente' also lives in this area. Al has scoliosis – a spectacular zig-zag bend in his spine, and a deep dent in his side (hence the name). He was probably born this way, but seems to do just fine. In good condition otherwise, he easily keeps up with the others. He can swim quite fast, often bowrides, but we've never seen him jump. We do know he has a healthy interest in sex!

It often takes us several hours to cover just a few miles, especially if the dolphins are busy and not easy to photograph. It's now hot, the sun high in a clear blue sky. Frying weather – we're grateful for the small sunshade on the boat and liberal applications of sunscreen. Just outside Peraki Bay we find a dolphin group containing another ID – one that we've known for years, but never had the chance to sex. To sex NZ dolphins you need to be a bit lucky. Often when they swim next to the boat they turn on their side, seemingly to have a look at us. Sometimes this gives us the glimpse that we need. If not, when they swim upside down at the surface, or lobtail upside down, or jump, we can usually get enough of a look to be sure of their gender.

A small underwater video camera, on a pole, works really well for this purpose. Another reliable and fun way to find out which dolphins are male and which are female is to get into the water. The dolphins need to be in the right 'mood', spending most of their time at the surface and associating closely with the boat. One of us, usually Liz, gets into a dive suit and hangs onto a rope attached to the bow of the boat. This provides a good view as the dolphins come to bowride, and is also an opportunity to take some video or still photographs. We do this at idle speed: any faster would put Liz in danger from the spinning propeller if she let go. This practice is risky, so, as they say on TV, 'don't try this at home'. When the boat is manoeuvred slowly among the dolphins, Liz gets a look at one we want to sex, and calls out that he is male. If the water is clear and the dolphins co-operative, we'll often take this in turns and try to get some underwater photographs. NZ dolphins are sometimes a little shy of free-swimming divers. Being slowly dragged on a rope behind a boat also works really well, and is much safer if you let go the rope!

Continuing on, we find a nursery group, four mothers and their calves, in mirror-calm water at Long Bay. Unusually, they are not at all shy and readily come over to investigate the boat, as if showing their calves what boats are like, that riding the bow can be fun, but that you must watch out for the spinning sharp thing at the back. One mum has a good fin nick, and her photograph adds to our database on how often females give birth. Back at base we'll be able to tell whether we've photographed her before, and whether she had a calf at that time.

With the mums and calves doing their own thing in the background, we turn off the engine for a lunch break: sandwiches and coffee. It's great to relax a bit in the sheltered bay, listening to the dolphins blowing nearby – hard to imagine a more peaceful setting. We often wonder what they would think of the fuss and acrimony over their protection. In this bay right now, these dolphins seem a lot more important than a few fishers who want to use gillnets rather than other fishing methods.

Lunch over, we leave the bay and realise that while it was windless in there, around the corner it is not. The typical summer northeasterly has gradually increased during the day. Squally Bay is living up to its name and is barely workable. Akaroa Harbour, where we came from, is definitely no longer workable. Twenty-five knots of northeasterly is funnelling down the harbour. Whitecaps everywhere mean that we can no longer spot dolphins reliably. We'll try to survey the harbour tomorrow, and perhaps the eastern side of the peninsula. Still, as we go 'off effort' for the bouncy eight-mile ride up the harbour, we reflect that it has been a good day. Seventy-seven dolphins seen, several identifiable dolphins photographed, including a mum that is probably a resighting, and one more ID sexed. That may seem slow progress to some. Dolphins don't give up their secrets easily; basic questions can take several years of research to answer.

After eight hours on the water (not a long day for us) we fuel up for tomorrow, give the outboard engine a rinse, and do a bit of routine maintenance to keep everything running well. We download the camera and the day's data from the boat computer to a laptop. This process takes only minutes, saves mind-numbing transcription of data sheets, and is error-free. So much better than in the early years of the study, when we had to spend several hours each day in a darkroom processing and printing the day's photographs.

For reliability's sake, all ID matching is done from good photographs rather than recognition of individuals at sea, but a quick look at the ID catalogue shows that we did indeed see that female before, with a newborn calf, three years ago. A year later she was with a one-year-old calf, and was alone the next year. Pretty normal really: most mature females have calves every 2–3 years.

A little more tidying up, washing the underwater camera and dive suits, recharging batteries in the cameras and other gear, and we are done for the day. Much more work will be needed back at university, matching all the pictures and analysing the data. Right now, sun and wind have taken their toll and neither of us has much energy left. Whose turn was it to cook dinner?

ACKNOWLEDGEMENTS

THIS BOOK grew from a research project we started in 1984. Beginning on a shoestring, the project slowly gathered momentum. We are especially grateful to our first sponsors: Project Jonah (NZ) Inc, Oceans Society (NZ), Cetacean Society International and IBM (NZ) Ltd. Greenpeace International, New Zealand Lottery Board, Project Jonah (NZ) Inc, World Wildlife Fund (NZ), Pacific Whale Foundation and IBM (NZ) Ltd provided funding at crucial stages. Creightons Naturally Pty, Neptune Aquasuits, Ocean Electronics, Tait Electronics, Hutchwilco, Neill Cropper and Co, David Reid Electronics and Tech Rentals very kindly sponsored or lent equipment for the study.

Since the 1990s, our research has been funded by grants from the Department of Conservation, Ministry of Fisheries, New Zealand Whale and Dolphin Trust, NABU International, Forest and Bird Protection Society, World Wildlife Fund, Reckitt and Colman, Hiking New Zealand, Hanimex and Wella.

Lots of people helped. Many fishers passed on dolphins they caught incidentally; we dissected these at the Lincoln Animal Health Laboratory, where the wonderful veterinary staff helped in many ways. We are very grateful for the collaborative efforts of our students and colleagues including Will Rayment, Trudi Webster, Sam du Fresne, Andrew Gormley, Stefan Bräger, Jennifer Turek, David Fletcher, William Thorpe, Frank Lad, Paul Wade, Jay Barlow, Barbara Taylor, Richard Barker and many others. Bertha Allison, Lloyd Whitten, Bill Rossiter, Barbara Maas and Hal Whitehead have been unflagging supporters.

We owe a special debt of gratitude to those who have worked hard for the dolphins' conservation, often battling against ignorance and unpleasantness. Hundreds of people have helped save NZ dolphins and protect the environment in which they live, including Kath and Brian Reid, Eugenie Sage, Barbara Leonard, Brian and Julie Fitness, Rebecca Bird, Barry Weeber, Kirsty Knowles, Katrina Subedar, Barbara Maas, Gemma McGrath, Sue Maturin, Davis Apiti, Peggy Oki, Mike Bossley, Ria Kemp, Christine Rose and Rio Rosselini. Of the politicians who have helped solve the conservation problems, Helen Clark, Pete Hodgson and Jim Anderton deserve honorable mention. Ron, Durelle, Paul and Vanetia Bingham, who started Black Cat Cruises, and Hugh and Pip Waghorn from Akaroa Dolphins, have helped in many ways. Huata Holmes helped us with the Māori names for NZ dolphin. We are very grateful to the team at Otago University Press.

DR STEVE DAWSON AND DR LIZ SLOOTEN,
University of Otago,
P.O. Box 56, Dunedin,
March 2013

FURTHER READING

MOST OF THE INFORMATION in this book is published in much more detail in scientific journals. These are often hard to get hold of and not easy to read. Indeed, our prime motivation for writing this book was to redress the lack of easily available information on NZ dolphins. For those who wish to chase up the details, here is a list of articles and books to get started with (references to further reading materials can be found within these). You will find these in the libraries of most universities in New Zealand and elsewhere.

Abel, R.S., Dobbins, A.G. and Brown, T. 1971. *Cephalorhynchus hectori* subsp. *bicolor* sightings, capture, captivity. *Investigations on Cetacea* III(1): 171–9.

Baker, A.N. 1978. The status of Hector's dolphin *Cephalorhynchus hectori* (van Beneden), in New Zealand waters. *Reports of the International Whaling Commission* 28: 331–34.

Baker, C.S., Hamner, R.M., Cooke, J., Heimeier, D., Vant, M., Steel, D., Constantine, R. 2012. Low abundance and probable decline of the critically endangered Maui's dolphin estimated by genotype capture-recapture. *Animal Conservation*, published online August 2012, doi:10.1111/j.1469-1795.2012.00590.x.

Bejder, L. and Dawson, S.M. 2001. Abundance, residency and habitat utilisation of Hector's dolphins in Porpoise Bay, New Zealand. *New Zealand Journal of Marine and Freshwater Research* 35: 277–87.

Bejder, L., Dawson, S.M. and Harraway, J. 1999. Responses of Hector's dolphins to boats and swimmers in Porpoise Bay. *New Zealand. Marine Mammal Science* 15(3): 738–50.

Bräger, S., Chong, A., Dawson, S.M., Slooten, E. and Würsig, B. 2000. A combined stereo-photogrammetry and underwater-video system to study group composition of dolphins. *Helgoland Marine Research* 53: 122–8.

Brakes, P. and Simmonds, M.P. 2011. *Whales and dolphins: cognition, culture, conservation and human perceptions*. Earthscan Publications Ltd, London.

Buckland, S.J., Hannah, D.J., Taucher, J.A., Slooten, E. and Dawson, S.M. 1990. Polychlorinated Dibenzo-p-dioxins and dibenzofurans in New Zealand's Hector's dolphin. *Chemosphere* 20: 1035–42.

Burkhart, S.M. and Slooten, E. 2003. Population viability analysis for Hector's dolphin (*Cephalorhynchus hectori*): A stochastic population model for local populations. *New Zealand Journal of Marine and Freshwater Research* 37: 553–66.

Cameron, C., Barker, R., Fletcher, D., Slooten, E. and Dawson, S. 1999. Modelling survival of Hector's dolphins around Banks Peninsula, New Zealand. *Journal of Agricultural, Biological and Environmental Statistics* 4(2): 126–35.

Cox, G.J. 1990. *Whale Watch: A Guide to New Zealand's Whales and Dolphins*. Collins, Auckland, New Zealand.

Currey, R.J.C., Boren, L.J., Sharp, B.R., Peterson, D. 2012. *A risk assessment of threats to Maui's dolphins*. Ministry for Primary Industries

and Department of Conservation, www.
doc.govt.nz/getting-involved/consultations/
current/threat-management-plan-review-
for-mauis-dolphin/

Dawson, S., Pichler, F., Slooten, E., Russell, K.
and Baker, C.S. 2001. The North Island
Hector's dolphin is vulnerable to extinction.
Marine Mammal Science 17(2): 366–71.

Dawson, S.M. 1988. The high-frequency
sounds of free-ranging Hector's dolphins
Cephalorhynchus hectori. *Reports of the
International Whaling Commission Special
issue* 9: 339–44.

Dawson, S.M. 1991. Clicks and Communication:
The behavioural and social contexts of
Hector's dolphin vocalisations. *Ethology*
88(4): 265–76.

Dawson, S.M. 1991. Incidental catch of Hector's
dolphins in inshore gillnets. *Marine Mammal
Science* 7(3): 283–95.

Dawson, S.M. 2003. Dolphins and whales,
in *The Natural History of Southern New
Zealand*, Darby, J.T., Fordyce, R.E, Mark, A.,
Probert, K., and Townsend, C.R. (eds), Otago
University Press, Dunedin, New Zealand, pp.
336–8.

Dawson, S.M. 2008. Marine Mammals, in *The
Natural History of Canterbury*, G. Knox and
Scott, R. (eds), Canterbury University Press,
Christchurch, New Zealand.

Dawson, S.M. and Slooten, E. 1996. *The
Downunder Dolphin: the story of Hector's
Dolphin*. Canterbury University Press,
Christchurch, New Zealand. 60 pp.

Dawson, S.M. and Slooten, E. 2005.
Management of gillnet bycatch of cetaceans
in New Zealand. *Journal of Cetacean
Research and Management* 7: 59–64.

Dawson, S.M. and Thorpe, C.W. 1990. A
quantitative analysis of the acoustic
repertoire of Hector's dolphin. *Ethology* 86:
131–45.

Dawson, S.M., and Slooten, E. 1993.
Conservation of Hector's dolphins: The case
and process which led to establishment
of the Banks Peninsula Marine Mammal
Sanctuary. *Aquatic Conservation* 3: 207–21.

Dawson, S.M., Read, A. and Slooten, E. 1998.
Pingers, porpoises and power: Uncertainties
with using pingers to reduce bycatch of
small cetaceans. *Biological Conservation*
84(2): 141–6.

Dawson, S.M., Slooten, E., DuFresne, S., Wade,
P. and Clement, D. 2004. Small-boat surveys
for coastal dolphins: Line-transect surveys
for Hector's dolphins (*Cephalorhynchus
hectori*). *Fishery Bulletin* 201: 441–51.

Dawson, S.M., Slooten, E., Fordyce, E. and
Rayment W. 2013. *Whales and Dolphins of
New Zealand*. Auckland University Press,
Auckland, New Zealand.

Dawson, S.M., Wade, P., Slooten, E. and Barlow,
J. 2008. Design and field methods for
sighting surveys of cetaceans in coastal
and riverine habitats. *Mammal Review* 38:
19–49.

Department of Conservation and Ministry
of Fisheries. 2007. Department of
Conservation, and Ministry of Agriculture
& Fisheries. Hector's dolphin threat
management discussion document, April
2007. Available at www.fish.govt.nz/en-nz/
Environmental.

Evans, P.G.H. 1987. *The Natural History of
Whales and Dolphins*. Christopher Helm,
London.

Gaskin, D.E. 1982. *The Ecology of Whales and
Dolphins*. Heinemann, London.

Gormley, A.M., Dawson, S.M., Slooten, E. and
Bräger, S. 2005. Capture-recapture estimates
of Hector's dolphin abundance at Banks
Peninsula, New Zealand. *Marine Mammal
Science* 21: 204–16.

Gormley, A.M., Slooten, E., Dawson, S.M., Barker, R.J., Rayment, W., du Fresne, S. and Bräger, S. 2012. First evidence that marine protected areas can work for marine mammals. *Journal of Applied Ecology* 49: 474–80.

Hamner, R.M., Oremus, M., Stanley, M., Brown, P., Constantine, R., Baker, C.S. 2012. *Estimating the abundance and effective population size of Maui's dolphins using microsatellite genotypes in 2010–11*. Department of Conservation Report available from www.doc.govt.nz

Harrison, R. and Bryden, M.M. 1988. *Whales, Dolphins and Porpoises*. Merehurst Press, London, UK.

Jones, P.D., Leathem, S.V., Hannah, D.J., and Day, P.J., et al. 1996. Biomagnification of PCBs and 2,3,7,8-substituted polychlorinated dibenzo-p-dioxins and dibenzofurans in New Zealand's Hector's dolphin. *Organohalogen Compounds* 29: 108–13.

Jones, P.D., Hannah, D.J., Buckland, S.J. and van Maanen, T., et al. 1999. Polychlorinated dibenzo-p-dioxins, dibenzofurans and polychlorinated in New Zealand cetaceans. *Journal of Cetacean Research and Management* (Special Issue 1): 157–67.

Leatherwood, S., Reeves, R.R. and Foster, L. 1983. *The Sierra Club Handbook of Whales and Dolphins*. Sierra Club Books, San Francisco.

Martien, K.K., Taylor, B.L., Slooten, E. and Dawson, S. 1999. A sensitivity analysis to guide research and management for Hector's dolphin. *Biological Conservation* 90: 183–91.

Ministry for Primary Industry and Department of Conservation. 2012. *Review of the Maui's dolphin Threat Management Plan*, Consultation Paper. Ministry for Primary Industries and Department of Conservation, Joint discussion paper No: 2012/18, www.doc.govt.nz/getting-involved/consultations/current/threat-management-plan-review-for-mauis-dolphin/

Norris, K.S. and Nicklin, F. 1992. Dolphins in crisis. *National Geographic* 182(3): 2–35.

Perrin, W.F., Würsig, B. and Thewissen, J.G.M. 2009. *Encyclopedia of Marine Mammals*, 2nd edn. Academic Press, San Diego.

Pichler, F., Baker, C.S., Dawson, S.M. and Slooten, E. 1998. Geographic isolation of Hector's dolphin populations described by mitochondrial DNA sequences. *Conservation Biology* 12(3): 676–82.

Pichler, F.B., Slooten, E. and Dawson, S.M. 2003. Hector's dolphins and fisheries in New Zealand: a species at risk?, in *Marine mammals and humans: towards a sustainable balance*, N.J. Gales, M.A. Hindell and R. Kirkwood (eds). CSIRO, Collingwood, Victoria, pp. 153–73.

Rayment, W., Dawson, S.M. and Slooten, E. 2009. Trialling an automated passive acoustic detector (T-POD) with Hector's dolphins (*Cephalorhynchus hectori*). *Journal of the Marine Biological Association* 89: 1015–22.

Rayment, W., Clement, D., Dawson, S., Slooten, E., and Secchi, E. 2011. Distribution of Hector's dolphins (*Cephalorhynchus hectori*) off the west coast, South Island, New Zealand, with implications for the management of bycatch. *Marine Mammal Science* 27: 398–420.

Rayment, W., Dawson, S., Scali, S. and Slooten, E. 2011. Listening for a needle in a haystack: Passive acoustic detection of dolphins at very low densities. *Endangered Species Research* 14: 149–56.

Rayment, W., Dawson, S.M. and Slooten, E. 2010. Seasonal changes in distribution of Hector's dolphin at Banks Peninsula, New

Zealand: implications for protected area design. *Aquatic Conservation: Marine and Freshwater Ecosystems* 20: 106–16.

Rayment, W., Dawson, S.M. and Slooten, E. 2010. Use of T-PODs for acoustic monitoring of *Cephalorhynchus* dolphins: A case study with Hector's dolphins in a marine protected area. *Endangered Species Research* 10: 333–9.

Rayment, W., Dawson, S.M., Slooten, E., Bräger, S., DuFresne, S. and Webster, T. 2009. Kernel density estimates of alongshore home range of Hector's dolphins (*Cephalorhynchus hectori*) at Banks Peninsula. *Marine Mammal Science* 25: 537–56.

Slooten, E. 1991. Age, growth and reproduction in Hector's dolphins. *Canadian Journal of Zoology* 69: 1689–1700.

Slooten, E. 1994. Behavior of Hector's dolphin: Classifying behavior by sequence analysis. *Journal of Mammalogy* 75: 956–64.

Slooten, E. 2007. Conservation management in the face of uncertainty: Effectiveness of four options for managing Hector's dolphin bycatch. *Endangered Species Research* 3: 169–79.

Slooten, E. 2011. The nature of whales and dolphins, in *Whales and dolphins: cognition, culture, conservation and human perceptions*, Brakes, P. and Simmonds, M.P. (eds). Earthscan Publications Ltd, London.

Slooten, E. and Davies, N. 2011. Hector's dolphin risk assessments: Old and new analyses show consistent results. *Journal of the Royal Society of New Zealand* 42: 49–60.

Slooten, E. and Dawson, S.M. 1994. Hector's Dolphin *Cephalorhynchus hectori*, in *Handbook of Marine Mammals*, Vol V, (Delphinidae and Phocoenidae), S.H Ridgway and R. Harrison (eds). Academic Press, New York, pp. 311–33

Slooten, E. and Dawson, S.M. 1995. Conservation of marine mammals in New Zealand. *Pacific Conservation Biology* 2: 64–76.

Slooten, E. and Dawson, S.M. 2008. Sustainable levels of human impact for Hector's dolphin. *The Open Conservation Biology Journal* 2: 37–43.

Slooten, E. and Dawson, S.M. 2010. Assessing the effectiveness of conservation management decisions: Likely effects of new protection measures for Hector's dolphin. *Aquatic Conservation: Marine and Freshwater Ecosystems* 20: 334–47.

Slooten, E. and Lad, F. 1991. Population biology and conservation of Hector's dolphin. *Canadian Journal of Zoology* 69: 1701–7.

Slooten, E., Dawson, S.M. and Lad, F. 1992. Survival rates of photographically identified Hector's dolphins from 1984 to 1988. *Marine Mammal Science* 8(4): 327–43.

Slooten, E., Dawson, S.M. and Rayment, W.J. 2004. Aerial surveys for coastal dolphins: Abundance of Hector's dolphins off the South Island west coast, New Zealand. *Marine Mammal Science* 20: 447–90.

Slooten, E., Dawson, S.M. and Whitehead, H. 1993. Associations among photographically identified Hector's dolphins. *Canadian Journal of Zoology* 71: 2311–18.

Slooten, E., Dawson, S.M., Rayment, W.J. and Childerhouse, S.J. 2006. A new abundance estimate for Maui's dolphin: What does it mean for managing this critically endangered species? *Biological Conservation* 128: 576–81.

Slooten, E., Dawson, S.M., Rayment, W.J. and Childerhouse, S.J. 2005. Distribution of Maui's dolphin, *Cephalorhynchus hectori maui*. *New Zealand Fisheries Assessment Report* 2005/28, 21pp. Ministry of Fisheries, Wellington.

Slooten, E., Fletcher, D. and Taylor, B.L.
2000. Accounting for uncertainty in risk
assessment: Case study of Hector's dolphin
mortality due to gillnet entanglement.
Conservation Biology 14: 1264–70.

Szabo, M. and Grace, R. 1992. Symphony of the
dolphins. *New Zealand Geographic* 14(2):
100–125.

Thorpe, C.W. and Dawson, S.M. 1991.
Automatic measurement of descriptive
features of Hector's dolphin vocalizations.
Journal of the Acoustical Society of America
89(1): 435–43.

Thorpe, C.W., Bates, R.H.T. and Dawson, S.M.
1991. Intrinsic echolocation capability of
Hector's dolphin Cephalorhynchus hectori.
Journal of the Acoustical Society of America
90(6): 2931–4.

Todd, Barbara. 1991. *Whales and dolphins of
Kaikoura, New Zealand*. Nature Downunder
and Craig Potton Publishing, Nelson.

Watson, L. 1981. *Sea Guide to the Whales of the
World*. Hutchinson, London.

Webster, T.A., Dawson, S.M. and Slooten, E.
2009. Evidence of sex segregation in Hector's
dolphin *(Cephalorhynchus hectori)*. *Aquatic
Mammals* 35(2): 212–19.

Webster, T.A., Dawson, S.M. and Slooten, E.
2010. A simple laser photogrammetry
technique for measuring Hector's dolphins
(Cephalorhynchus hectori) in the field.
Marine Mammal Science 26: 296–308.

INDEX

Page numbers in **bold** refer to illustrations.